What Do You Really Want?

HOW TO SET A GOAL AND GO FOR IT!

A GUIDE FOR TEENS

What Do You Really Want?

HOW TO SET A GOAL AND GO FOR IT!

A GUIDE FOR TEENS

Beverly K. Bachel

free spirit
PUBLISHING®

Works for kids®

Library of Congress Cataloging-in-Publication Data
Bachel, Beverly K., 1957–
    What do you really want? : how to set a goal and go for it! : a guide for teens / by Beverly K. Bachel.
        p. cm.
    Includes bibliographical references and index.
    ISBN 1-57542-085-6 (pbk. : alk. paper)
    1. Goal (Psychology)—Juvenile literature. 2. Planning—Juvenile literature. 3. Success—Psychological aspects—Juvenile literature. [1. Goal (Psychology) 2. Success.] I. Title.

BF505.G6 B33 2001
153.8—dc21   00-057286

At the time of this book's publication, all facts and figures cited are the most current available; all telephone numbers, addresses, and Web site URLs are accurate and active; all publications, organizations, Web sites, and other resources exist as described in this book; and all have been verified. The author and Free Spirit Publishing make no warranty or guarantee concerning the information and materials given out by organizations or content found at Web sites, and we are not responsible for any changes that occur after this book's publication. If you find an error or believe that a resource listed here is not as described, please contact Free Spirit Publishing. Parents, teachers, and other adults: We strongly urge you to monitor children's use of the Internet.

Edited by Jana Branch, Darsi Dreyer, and Elizabeth Verdick
Cover design by Percolator
Interior design and illustrations by Marieka Heinlen
Index compiled by Randl Ockey

10 9 8 7 6 5 4 3 2
Printed in the United States of America

Free Spirit Publishing Inc.
217 Fifth Avenue North, Suite 200
Minneapolis, MN 55401-1299
(612) 338-2068
help4kids@freespirit.com
www.freespirit.com

To all my guardian angels—especially Jim, Vi, and Valeria.

CONTENTS

LIST OF REPRODUCIBLE PAGES

A Note from Ann Bancroft

I grew up loving the outdoors. When I was eight, I led my own mini-expeditions, convincing my cousins to go with me on backyard camping trips in the middle of winter. At twelve, I learned about Sir Ernest Shackleton's legendary 1914 Antarctic voyage on the ship the *Endurance,* which became trapped in sea ice just one day's sail from the continent. The ship eventually sank, leaving its crew stranded for nearly two years. From then on, I knew I wanted to be a polar explorer.

As a teen, my goal was to go to college and become a teacher. As a student with dyslexia (a learning difference), school wasn't easy for me. In fact, some days felt like a torment. But my goal to teach kept me focused on the future.

Today, I'm both a teacher and an explorer (I'm the first woman to ski across the ice to both the North and South Poles). I had to overcome a lot of obstacles along the way to my goals, but I'm living my dream and doing what I feel I was meant to do. And I know *you* can as well.

No matter how impossible it may seem some days, you really *do* have the power to set your own course. It's not easy, but it's always rewarding. And your achievements—no matter how big or small—will stay with you your entire life.

If I could offer you only one piece of advice, it would be this: never accept "no" when it comes to pursuing your dreams. Believe in yourself and what you want to do, so you can get what you really want out of life. The skills you'll learn from this book—including how to set goals, build a support team, and keep yourself motivated—will help you as you set your course and explore where life takes you.

Whatever your dream, remember that you've got what it takes to achieve it. Now, get going!

Ann Bancroft is the founder and leader of the Ann Bancroft Foundation *(www.annbancroftfoundation.org),* a nonprofit organization that celebrates the achievements of women and girls. As a result of Ann's successes and achievements on her polar expeditions, she has become a sought-after school speaker and seminar leader on the topics of teamwork, leadership, and goal setting. Ann is also a former school teacher and coach.

INTRODUCTION

Do you have dreams and wishes? Everyone does. It's fun to imagine the amazing things you might achieve someday. But what about today? Are you doing anything right now to make your dreams and wishes come true? When you hear yourself saying, "I wish . . ." or "I dream about . . ." or "I really hope . . . ," it's time to ask:

Do I only wish it or do I want it to be real?

Can you make your dreams and wishes real? The answer is a definite yes. How do you do it? By setting goals.

What's a Goal?

A goal is something you *want*, of course! But there's more to it than that. A goal is also something you're willing to work for—whether it takes you days, weeks, months, or years to achieve. Maybe you want to develop a new habit or break an old one. Maybe you want to make the team or make better grades or make new friends. Maybe you want to travel, go to college, get a summer job, or change the world for the better. Goals are as individual as the people who set them. The important thing is that your goals hold meaning for *you.*

So, what's the difference between a dream and a goal? A dream is something in your mind and in your heart—where it will stay forever unless you bring it to life. A goal, like a dream, is something you desire. But a goal is more specific, more defined, more measurable than a dream. In fact, goals can be stepping stones to your dreams.

What if you've never had many (or any) goals? What if you've had goals before but never reached them? There's good news. You can

1

learn to set and reach goals—even if you haven't had much experience or success with this before. Like any other skill, the earlier you start goal setting and the more you practice, the easier it gets.

I believe that you have the power to create your own best future. No matter who you are or where you come from, you can get what you really want out of life. You can make your dreams come true. And this book will tell you how.

About This Book

When I was a teen, I had lots of dreams. I knew there were thousands of possibilities out there, but I wasn't sure how to make them happen. I wish someone had shown me how to set goals. It wasn't until I was an adult that I understood that goal setting is something you can learn on your own.

This book explains the why, what, and how of goal setting, so you can reach goals yourself. You'll discover why goals matter, what they can do for you, and how to make them a part of your life. Throughout the book, you'll find advice, tips, and words of wisdom from teens and adults who've used goal setting to improve their lives. You'll also find plenty of reproducible forms that you can photocopy and fill out on your own. These forms help you figure out and plan your goals, write them down, and most importantly, *go after them!* Even if you're tempted to write directly in this book (which you should NEVER do if it's from the library), photocopy the pages instead. This way, you can rework them if you need to—or do them again and again for each and every goal. A copy machine may be found at your school, public library, or local copy shop. If you have access to a computer, you could even use a scanner.

How do I know that the principles in this book work? Because I've used them to reach my own goals. From making new friends to buying my first car, from improving my golf game to starting a business, I've used goal setting to accomplish all sorts of things, including writing this book (which for me is a dream come true).

While writing *What Do You Really Want?*, I talked with teens who live in small towns, big cities, and rural areas across the United States to find out about their dreams and goals. Their aspirations, personalities, and outlooks on life are as unique as their schools, families, friendships, and communities. As I discovered, no two of the teens are alike, but they share enthusiasm and a strong commitment to improving their lives and their world. You can use their stories (I call them "Goal Getters in Action") as inspiration to get more out of life yourself.

What goals will you set for yourself in the coming months? What hurdles will you have to overcome to reach them? Who will you turn to if you need help? How will you celebrate when you accomplish each goal? And then, what new goals will you set? There's no way to know without diving in and getting started.

Along the way, I'd like to hear about your questions or the goals you're pursuing. Feel free to write to me!

Beverly K. Bachel
c/o Free Spirit Publishing
217 Fifth Avenue North, Suite 200
Minneapolis, MN 55401-1299

email: help4kids@freespirit.com

FIRST THINGS FIRST: WHY GOALS MATTER

How did a ten-year-old girl turn her dream of giving free suitcases to 300 foster kids in her community into an international organization that has given away more than 300,000 suitcases around the world?

How did a teenage boy recruit more than 20,000 high school students as "book buddies" to work with elementary school students who wanted to improve their reading skills?

What motivated a nine-year-old girl who loved baseball to become the first girl in her community to try out for a Little League team, and then convince sixteen other girls to join her? And how did she earn a black belt in Tae Kwon Do and nine varsity athletic letters, and volunteer hundreds of hours to projects in her community—all before graduating from high school?

The answer? Goal setting. And *you* can do it the way *they* did it.

Ask any successful adult or teen, "How did you get where you are in life?" and chances are, he or she will say that setting goals was the key. Why are goals so important? Check out the Top 10 List of reasons that begins on page 5.

Top 10 List
(Why Goals Are Worth Having)

1. **They help you be who you want to be.** You can have all the dreams in the world, but if you don't *act* on them, how will you get where you want to go? When you know how to set a goal and go for it, you chart a path of action that takes you step by step toward the future you want.

2. **They stretch your comfort zone.** Goals involve a few risks (the healthy kind). In pursuit of a goal, you may find yourself talking to new people, trying out for a team, performing on stage, making a speech, or doing something else that draws people's attention. Pushing yourself past your normal comfort zone is a great way to grow.

3. **They boost your confidence.** When you set a goal and reach it, you prove to yourself and others that you've got what it takes to get things done. Goals not only make you stronger—they help you feel good about yourself, too.

"The larger the goal, the greater my feeling of triumph."
JESSICA, 15

4. **They give your life purpose.** Goals show you—and the world— what you value. They also give you a sense of direction. When you're going after your goals, you're less likely to spend your days feeling bored or wasting your time.

5. **They help you rely on yourself.** You don't have to let other people decide your life for you. You can take charge of your life by setting goals and making a plan to reach them. Once you get

into the goal-setting habit, you'll notice that you feel a lot more independent. (And the people around you will notice your new independence, too!)

"I know having goals makes my parents proud of me. They see how hard I work to reach my goals and how responsible I am. As a result, they trust me more." ERIC, 15

6. **They encourage you to trust your decisions.** You're at a point in your life where you're making more decisions at home and at school. Sometimes, it's really easy to go along with the crowd or be swayed by what other people want you to do. But when you keep your goals in mind, your choices will become clearer. You'll learn to trust your decisions, because they're right for *you.*

7. **They help you turn the impossible into the possible.** Goal setting breaks down seemingly out-of-reach dreams into small, manageable, and practical steps. You can turn your "someday" dreams into real-life accomplishments.

8. **They prove that you can make a difference.** Are your goals about changing your own life? Are they about changing the lives of others and improving the world? Whether you want to make a difference in your own life or in someone else's, goal setting helps you achieve what you set out to do—one step at a time.

9. **They improve your outlook on life.** Goals help you move forward—a positive direction to be going. (Much better than sitting still or getting nowhere at all.) This momentum is a real energizer. You'll feel more positive, guaranteed.

10. **They lead to feelings of satisfaction.** Studies have shown that people who set and reach goals perform at higher levels, are more satisfied with themselves, and achieve more. In fact, if you look

at the goal setters you know or admire (friends, family members, teachers, business owners, community leaders, athletes, celebrities), you'll probably see people who are proud of their success and eager to keep aiming for more in life.

"There's no greater feeling than setting a goal and accomplishing it. When you do, you've got something that will last the rest of your life." PETTUS, 18

3 Goal Myths (Don't Believe Them for a Second)

Myth #1: "Who needs goals? I'll be fine without them."
Wrong! Success doesn't just happen by accident or sheer luck. It's more often the result of hard work. Striving to meet a goal can be a very satisfying process. You might even find that having a goal gives you extra energy to put forth your best effort.

Myth #2: "I have to wait 'til January 1 to set goals."
Contrary to what a lot of people think, the start of a new year isn't the best or only time to begin making changes or setting goals. There's no time like the present. If you start now, you're that much closer to making your dreams a reality.

Myth #3: "I have to do it all by myself."
It's true that reaching a goal is a personal process. But this doesn't mean you can't ask for help when you need it. Believe it or not, people in your life (family, friends, teachers, coaches) will most likely want to help in any way they can. Knowing you've got support can make the pursuit of a goal even more exciting.

3 Goal Truths

1. **Goals work.**

2. **Not enough people have them.**

3. **You can be someone who does have goals—a Goal Getter!**

Now that you've got the facts, are you ready to learn more about goals? First you'll need one very important tool: a Goal Tracker. It can be a blank book, spiral notebook, sketchpad, or three-ring binder—anything that lets you record information on paper and store it in a safe place.

One of the keys to successful goal setting is *the written word.* Writing your goals on paper—instead of just keeping them in your head—helps you clarify your thinking and commit to success. And that's what your Goal Tracker is for: writing it all down.

I recommend a Goal Tracker that has enough paper for you to create two separate sections. (You may even want to use a subject notebook that has dividers and pockets for extra storage.) You'll use the first section of your Goal Tracker for completing the reproducible forms that you photocopy from this book. Depending on what kind of Goal Tracker you choose, you can copy the reproducible pages and:

1. tape or glue them so they stick

2. store them in the pockets

3. use a hole-punch so they stay in a binder

Or, if you prefer, copy them by hand into your Goal Tracker.

The second section will be for journaling. If you already keep a journal, you probably know that writing about your thoughts, feelings, ideas, and experiences is a great way to get to know yourself better. Lots of teens keep journals to explore what's going on in their lives and work through problems. When setting goals, it's helpful to use a journal as a personal resource.

In it, you can write about:

- why a particular goal has meaning for you
- how you felt before and after taking action
- problems you're facing and how you want to handle them
- ideas and feelings you want to keep to yourself
- anything that's on your mind

The journaling section is separate, so you have the freedom to scribble, doodle, express ideas, write random thoughts, rant and rave, or do whatever else you're in the mood to do. You can be as messy or as neat as you want. And you can tear out any pages that you don't feel like keeping. Don't worry about spelling, grammar, punctuation, or anything else that might slow you down. The purpose of journaling is to express yourself in a way that's comfortable. No one else has to read what you write, unless you want them to.

"I keep a journal, although I don't write in it every day. I get a kick out of looking back, even to a month before, and seeing where I was then and where I am now." REBECCA, 18

"I use my journal to write about my feelings, especially when I'm upset or angry about something. Sometimes I even use it to write poetry." MICHAEL S., 17

"I write about the things that happen in my life, especially when things aren't going well. And then I write about what I can do to make them better." JAIMA, 14

Throughout this book, you'll find lots of "Think It & Ink It" exercises for the journal section of your Goal Tracker. I encourage you to give all of them—and the reproducible forms—a try. The forms are specially designed to help you clarify your dreams and goals, plan them out, and stay on the Goal-Getter path. The journaling exercises are meant to help you take a closer look at yourself, and they don't take long to complete. If you prefer not to keep a journal, that's fine, too. Instead, concentrate on the first section of your Goal Tracker, which is the most important part.

Once you've started your Goal Tracker, try the following tips to help you get the most out of it:

1. **Experiment.** Try different notebook options until you find a Goal Tracker that feels right to you.

2. **Date your entries.** The dates give you reference points that help you chart your progress. You'll be amazed when you look back and see how much you've accomplished.

3. **Use it often.** The more you put into your Goal Tracker, the more you'll get out of it. You can use it every day, if you'd like.

4. **Create an "ideas" page.** Jot down things you want to learn more about, questions you want to ask others or find answers to, and ideas for activities you'd like to try.

5. **Review it every few weeks.** Look back at ideas you wrote down weeks ago. They might take on new meaning in light of what you're doing today.

6. **Be creative.** You're free to personalize your Goal Tracker with photos, drawings, quotes, or whatever else will make it your own. After copying the reproducible forms, fill them out in different colors of ink, if you'd like, or have fun decorating them.

If you're not sure whether a Goal Tracker will be helpful to you, test it out for a few weeks anyway. You'll probably discover that the process of writing, drawing, recording, and imagining will give you insight that you couldn't get any other way. Putting pen to paper on a regular basis can empower you, enlighten you, and keep you focused on success. Try it!

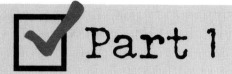

Part 1

DISCOVER WHAT YOU REALLY WANT

What Are Your Dreams?

"It's the possibility of having a dream come true that makes life interesting."—Paulo Coelho

Every day, you're bombarded with hundreds of messages telling you what you should want and who you should be. Family, friends, teachers, magazines, TV, radio, the Internet, and billboards give you plenty of "advice": Do this. Say that. Be this. Want that. Many people go through life listening too closely to these messages. It's easy to forget that the most meaningful dreams and wishes don't come from outside sources—they come from within you.

Exploring your dreams and wishes—even the ones that seem impossible and out of reach—helps you begin to design the future you want. Ask yourself, "What do I really want?" and listen to what you have to say. This conversation with yourself may be the most important (and the most challenging) one you'll ever have. *Do I want to be a person known for helping others? For being trustworthy? For being adventurous? Do I want to stand up for myself more strongly? Be able to handle my feelings better? Experience new things? Do I want to be an honor roll student, a baseball player, an artist, or an engineer? Do I want to try out for the school play or start a new club?* Take some time to think about what's right for you.

Maybe you've got an answer right away: *I want to be a rock star . . . I want to see the world . . . I want to be class president . . . I want to succeed in school . . . I want to be admired . . .* Or maybe you don't have any answers at all. Either way, it's time to dig a little deeper—to find out what you truly long for and wish for yourself . . . and why.

To get started, answer the questions on form #1, "What Inspires Me?" on page 13, which you can photocopy for your Goal Tracker. This will help you understand what your sources of inspiration really are.

What Inspires Me?

Photocopy for your
Goal Tracker!!!

• What do I enjoy doing? Why?

• What don't I enjoy doing? Why?

• What do I like to read about?

• What gives meaning and purpose to my life?

• What are my talents or skills? How might I improve them?

• What do I most often daydream about?

THINK IT & INK IT

When you were younger, what were some of your hopes and dreams? How have your hopes and dreams changed in the past two years? In the past year? How have *you* changed? How do you think you'll change in the next two years? In the next five years? Write about these ideas in the journal section of your Goal Tracker.

On pages 15–16, you'll find form #2, called "Dream Starters," which contains questions to help you start thinking about what you really want for yourself and your future. Photocopy the form for your Goal Tracker. You can fill in all five of the Dream Starters, or whichever ones capture your imagination. Keep your answers to yourself or talk about them with your friends.

The Dream Starters are designed to help you dream on the page. As you write down your dreams, they take shape in your mind and grow more powerful. This process of expressing your dreams in words can lead you to feel as if your dreams really are within your reach.

Photocopy for your Goal Tracker!!!

Dream Starters

Dream Starter #1: Write about three people you know and admire (such as friends, family members, teachers, coaches, neighbors). What do they do that you think is great? What makes them special?

Dream Starter #2: Write about three people you admire but haven't met (for example, celebrities, leaders, athletes, artists, historical figures). What have they done that you think is great? What makes them special to you?

Dream Starter #3: Imagine it's graduation night. Just before you head into the auditorium, you're handed a sheet of paper and asked to write five predictions about things you expect to accomplish or become. Write about your predictions.

Dream Starter #4: Imagine you're getting ready for your five-year high school reunion. You've been asked to make a five-minute video about your life since graduation. Write about what you'll put in your video.

Dream Starter #5: Imagine you're seventy years old, and your friends are about to honor you with a Lifetime Achievement Award. What will they say about you? What did you do in your life that they think is special? Did you go to college? Create art? Start a business? Were you generous to your friends? Committed to a cause?

The Dream Starters can also help you understand your *values*—what you believe in, what's important to you deep down. Even if you're not aware of your values, they help motivate you, and they play a big part in what you want. If you're tuned in to your values, they can become a guiding force in your life.

Take another look at your completed Dream Starters pages. Suppose you wrote something like this for Dream Starter #2:

"Michael Jordan is one of my heroes. Not just cause he's an incredible basketball player (the best in the world), but because he keeps believing in himself no matter what. Nearly everyone knows he was cut from his junior high basketball team. But he didn't give up. When he decided to try to play baseball after he was already a basketball star, people thought he was crazy. He did it anyway and even though he didn't make the pros, he was glad he gave baseball a try. That's pretty cool."

What might this passage say about you and your dreams and values? On the surface, one might guess that you enjoy sports, admire athletes who've accomplished amazing feats, and perhaps even dream of being a successful athlete yourself someday. But going deeper, one might notice that you respect people who have a strong sense of self—who believe in themselves, even when the odds (and popular opinion) are against them. This might show that you *value* self-esteem, self-respect, hard work, and the ability to take healthy risks. Look more closely at your finished Dream Starters to see if you can begin to identify what you really value.

Nearly every choice you make is influenced by your values. In fact, what you believe in or don't believe in helps you decide how to spend your time, who to spend it with, and how much energy to put into an activity. If you value having a close family, you'll try to be there for your family members when they need you. If you value helping your community, you'll most likely volunteer your time and skills. In this way, values help guide how you live your life.

Some of your values might express a connection you have to other people or things such as:

- family
- friends
- education
- community
- animals

- the environment
- culture
- sports
- music
- art

Some of your values might express the kind of person you'd like to be or the way you'd like others to see you:

- respectful
- hardworking
- capable
- loving
- helpful
- honest

- dependable
- independent
- inquisitive
- healthy
- creative

To figure out what some of your values are, review the answers you wrote on the Dream Starters form. Now ask yourself the following: *Who or what do I really care about? What holds meaning for me?*

Hidden in the answers to these questions are your values. And these values are, in part, what drive your dreams.

Here's what some teens have to say about their values:

"I want to be a loyal and trustworthy friend. That's why I try to never talk about my friends behind their backs."

JAIMA, 14

"I really believe in the U.S. Constitution, particularly the right to free speech. I'm interested in politics and hope to run for public office one day." MATT, 12

"More than anything else, I want to help other people. I'd like to go to college and major in social work. Then, I'd like to buy an apartment building where homeless people could live. I'd also like to become a cosmetologist so I could style people's hair and help them feel good about themselves." SHAKEILA, 16

"I want compassion to be the guide in my life, to be a part of everything I do." THIEN, 19

"I value the outdoors. As a result, I spend a lot of time outside and do things to help the environment." DELFINO, 14

Do these teens share some of your values? Have their words helped you figure out some of what you believe in—what holds meaning for you?

You can use form #3, "Values That Matter to Me," on pages 20–21 to learn more about yourself and your values. Photocopy it, fill it out, and store it in your Goal Tracker so you can refer to it often.

Photocopy for your
Goal Tracker!!!

Values That Matter to Me

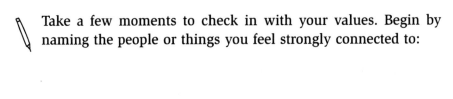

Take a few moments to check in with your values. Begin by naming the people or things you feel strongly connected to:

Next, pick three of them to write about. Ask yourself: Why do I feel connected to this person or thing?

1.

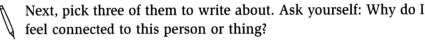

2.

3.

Think about the personal qualities that you believe are important for you to have. Write about them here:

 Based on what you've written so far, list one to three values that are important to you. Remember, your values are the ideas or things that really matter to you:

1.

2.

3.

THINK IT & INK IT

Choose three values that you hold and write about ways you demonstrate them to others. Or try writing a Code of Conduct for how you'd like to live your life. For example, if you value being friendly and caring, your Code of Conduct might include the following:

- Smile when I say "Good morning" to my family.

- Say encouraging things to my friends.

- Be kind to all people and animals.

Write your ideas in the journal section of your Goal Tracker.

Values and Dreams Are Connected

To think more specifically about your dreams and why they're mean-ingful to you, turn on your favorite music, close your eyes, and ask yourself *exactly* what you want to do with your life now and in the future. If you were given the opportunity to do *anything*, what would you do—and why?

Think about what you can accomplish relatively quickly, such as finishing a history report or completing a job application. Next con-sider things that might take a little longer, either because they won't happen until you're older or because they require more work, such as getting a part in a play, qualifying for a college scholarship, or buying your first car. Then think about things that aren't likely to happen for years; for example, producing your first album, becoming a doctor, or starting a family of your own. Finally, imagine the seemingly impos-sible like competing in the Olympics, sitting on the U.S. Supreme Court, or becoming a translator for the United Nations.

On page 24 is form #4, "Dare to Dream," which you can photo-copy and place in your Goal Tracker. Complete the sentence starter at the top of the form by making a list of all the things you'd like to do.

Write as quickly as you can for five to ten minutes. Try to come up with at least ten things. Don't be concerned about whether your ideas seem silly, out of reach, or extravagant. Write down anything and everything that crosses your mind, without worrying about how you'll accomplish it. Pretend you have an endless supply of whatever you need—talent, money, time, motivation, and help from others. Writing down your dreams on paper helps to make them real, because they become something tangible and concrete—something you and others can see and touch. Then, you can write about how reaching those dreams might make you feel inside.

When you're done with "Dare to Dream," you can talk with your friends about what you wrote and encourage them to make their own lists. After everyone has created a list, share what you wrote with each other, if you feel comfortable doing so. This is a great way to be inspired by your friends and their dreams.

You can also talk to the adults in your life to find out what their dreams are now and what their dreams were when they were younger. You may discover some surprising information about people when you start talking about their values and dreams. Form #5, "Conversation Starters," on page 25 provides several opening lines that you can try. There's space for taking notes during your conversations, too.

THINK IT & INK IT

What are your talents and your strengths? Think about them and what you like to do. How might your talents and strengths become a part of your future? Spend some time writing about this topic in the journal section of your Goal Tracker.

Dare to Dream

> "To accomplish great things, we must not only act,
> but also dream."—Anatole France

✎ If I could do anything, I would:

✎ Reaching my dreams would help me to feel:

Form #5
Date: _____

Conversation Starters

Photocopy for your
Goal Tracker!!!

Ask these questions of friends, family members, or other people in your life.

• What matters to you more than anything else?

• Which of your dreams gets you really inspired?

• If you could do anything, what would it be? Why?

• How are your dreams connected to your values?

• When you were my age, what was the one thing you most wanted to do?

• What values do you see in me?

Here's what some teens had to say about their dreams:

I want to . . .

"Start a band with my friends." CARLEEN, 12

"Open my own restaurant." MEGHAN, 15

"Be a kindergarten teacher." YOUA, 11

"Be a movie star." FERNANDO, 17

"Get a master's degree in computer engineering." MATT, 12

"Work as a biologist or a scientist." ABIGAIL, 12

"Buy a crushed-velvet cloak." PATTI, 16

"Work as an airplane mechanic." TEGAN, 12

"Be a professional fisherman." TOMMY, 13

"Not miss any school." MELISSA, 16

"Work with Nelson Mandela." REBECCA, 18

"Join the Air Force Academy and fly fighter jets." BEN, 13

Do any of these dreams resemble yours? Or are these dreams completely different from yours? Do any of these dreams get you thinking in new directions?

THINK IT & INK IT

How do your values and dreams differ from those of your friends? How are they the same? What are some ways your friends help you live by your values and support your dreams? Do your friends ever try to hold you back, and if so, how do you feel about it and deal with it? Use the journal section of your Goal Tracker to explore these ideas.

GOAL GETTERS IN ACTION

ALISON grew up in a small town in northern Minnesota. She loved baseball and dreamed about playing on a Little League team. Her town had only one team, but there weren't any girls on it. At age nine, Alison summoned her courage and tried out anyway. She made the team but was often teased, and that made the year tougher than she had expected. Rather than quit, she convinced sixteen other girls to join the team the next summer. Today, girls are a big part of Little League teams in the area, and Alison continues to serve as a positive role model when it comes to sports. She earned a black belt in Tae Kwon Do when she was fourteen, and nine varsity athletic letters in high school. She's also committed to making a difference in her community. She's volunteered hundreds of hours to projects, including cleaning up roadside ditches and planting trees. And because her dream is to be a trauma surgeon, she volunteered on an eighteen-day medical mission to Honduras. After hearing Alison speak about her trip, five others from her small community were inspired to sign up for a similar mission. "I think that there is nothing greater in life than helping those around us who are worse off than ourselves," says Alison.

PETTUS, of Tuscaloosa, Alabama, grew up with a love for reading, and he wanted to help other kids discover the same excitement for books. His goal: to tap the vast high school talent pool to provide reading mentors and positive role models for young kids. When he was a junior, he created Read & Lead™, a program that pairs high school students as "book buddies" with elementary school students who want to improve their reading skills. After launching the program in his area, Pettus developed a brochure and a how-to manual, set up a Web site, and spoke about the program throughout the country. Thanks to Read & Lead, at least 20,000 high school students are now helping young children discover the joy of reading. Pettus, now eighteen, attributes Read & Lead's success to a simple dream: every single person helping at least one other person in some way. "I grew up setting goals," says Pettus. "At the beginning of each year, my parents and my sister and I wrote down our goals for the upcoming year. For as long as I can remember, I've been interested in helping others and have often set goals with this in mind." To find out more about Read & Lead, check out *www.readandlead.org.*

When she was ten years old, **AUBYN,** from Hickory, North Carolina, learned that most kids in foster care move three or four times. Some of them don't have any luggage, so they may carry their belongings in garbage bags. "I tried to put myself in their place and think how I would feel," says Aubyn. "I wanted to make them feel special by giving them something of their own to keep." With the help of a 4-H club, Boy Scouts, Girl Scouts, and local churches, she began collecting suitcases, hoping to give one to each of the 300 foster children in her county. Aubyn achieved that goal, but she didn't stop there. She founded Suitcases for Kids, an organization now active in all 50 states and in 27 countries. More than 300,000 suitcases have been given away, and Aubyn has personally cleaned more than 35,000 of them. In addition, she travels throughout the United States encouraging others to make a difference in their communities. To find out more, visit *www.suitcasesforkids.org.*

THINK IT & INK IT

Fast forward. Imagine it's 2025 and you've just achieved the seemingly impossible. You're now doing the very thing you've dreamed of. Write a letter to yourself at whatever age you are now offering advice and encouragement. Use the journal section of your Goal Tracker.

Your Dreamprint

> "Your imagination is your preview of life's coming attractions."—Albert Einstein

Another way to make your dreams more real is to create a Dreamprint. A Dreamprint is a collage (a collection of pictures, words, images, and objects) of all the things you value and wish for. It allows you to think in pictures instead of words. It's your own personal work of art that represents all the things you'd like to do with your life. Like a blueprint that puts an architect's dream on paper—where everyone can see it— your Dreamprint will help make your dreams more real by turning them into something you can actually see and touch.

What you'll need:

- magazines (with lots of pictures), catalogs, brochures, and other printed materials you can cut up
- scissors
- small objects related to your dreams (such as maps, theater tickets, a guitar pick)
- one or more pictures of yourself (photographs or drawings)
- posterboard or other heavy paper
- glue or tape

1. Cut out pictures from the magazines, catalogs, brochures, and other printed materials of things you'd like in your life or people  who represent the qualities you want to have. For instance, if you want a new bike, find a photo of a bike you'd like to own. If you dream of being a writer, cut out a picture of your favorite author.

2. Look for words, captions, quotes, and phrases that reflect characteristics you'd like to possess (bravery, intelligence, curiosity) or your philosophy toward life (to make the world a better place, continue to learn, care about others).

3. Sort through your pictures and objects, and set aside any that don't represent your *true* dreams and values.

4. Now it's time to assemble your Dreamprint. Put a picture of yourself in the center of a piece of posterboard or other heavy paper. Arrange the images, words, and objects around your picture however you like, and then glue or tape them in place.

5. Put your finished Dreamprint where you'll see it every morning when you wake up and every night before you go to sleep. You can also make a smaller version of your Dreamprint to store in your Goal Tracker, hang in your locker, tape to the bathroom mirror, carry in your backpack, or use as a bookmark, so you'll always be reminded of your dreams.

 GOAL GETTERS IN ACTION

When **JOEY** was eleven, he made a Dreamprint that helped motivate him to run several times a week to prepare for the annual "Race for the Cure" in his community. "I wanted to run in honor of my grandma who has breast cancer, but I'd never run that far before. My collage helped me believe that I could do it and that running a race was easy compared to everything my grandma was going through."

"I have my Dreamprint on my bulletin board. It says, 'I got to get a life,' and has little men running all over the place and clocks scattered everywhere. This is to remind me to do something important with my life and not get caught up in all the day-to-day trivial stuff." JULIA R., 17

"My collage is made of pictures of my dreams. I have it tacked up to my ceiling, so I can look at it every night before I go to sleep. It helps me get to bed thinking about all of my future goals. I also have very nice dreams as a result of looking at my collage before bed." CHINA, 14

You're on Your Way

"The future belongs to those who believe in the beauty of their dreams."—Eleanor Roosevelt

Now that you've put your dreams and values on paper, you're on your way to creating a better future for yourself. You've taken a big step because challenging yourself to think about what *you* want—not what other people want for you—is a key part of identifying what's most important to you in life. The more you think about what you want, the more your motivation grows, and the clearer your path will become. Let yourself dream, and then get ready to make it real with goal setting.

 Part 2

BECOME A
GOAL GETTER

The Long and Short of Goals

"If you don't know where you are going,
you might wind up someplace else."—Yogi Berra

In "Part 1: Discover What You Really Want," you found ways to let loose your wishes, hopes, and dreams. But how do you get from where you are today to a tomorrow where what you want has a chance of happening? By taking action. Sure, it would be nice if simply making a wish, or hoping for something good to happen, or spending lots of time dreaming would lead to a better future—but life doesn't work that way. It's up to us to make our dreams real.

In other words, you (or anyone else) can't just want something and expect to get it. Instead, you need to figure out how you're going to get it. This is where goal setting comes in. Your goals are the "how to" process for reaching your dreams.

Some goals can be achieved in a day, a week, or a month. These are called short-term goals. Others, such as being awarded MVP on your tennis team this season or reading several of Shakespeare's plays, may require a lot more time and effort. These are called long-term goals. Usually, long-term goals are broken down into several short-term goals that help you keep moving toward your main goal. So, in this sense, short-term goals can support your long-term ones.

But short-term goals don't always have to support a long-term goal. For example, you could decide that your goal is to finish your homework by the time your favorite TV show comes on this evening. Or you could have a goal of exercising for twenty-five minutes today. Setting and reaching small challenges like these can get you in a goal-setting frame of mind. If you'd like, you can focus on a few short-term goals until you feel inspired to work your way up to goals that require more time to complete.

GOAL GETTERS IN ACTION

When **THIEN** left Vietnam at age thirteen and arrived in the United States, she didn't know any English. But she came with a dream of becoming a doctor, so she could help others. Inspired by her grandmother, a highly respected herbal-medicine doctor in Vietnam, Thien began setting short-term goals. First, she tackled English by learning three or four new words a day. She did it by reading children's books and a dictionary, and by practicing her new words in conversations with friends. Thien's vocabulary grew quickly, giving her confidence to set and achieve other goals. Today, at nineteen, she's on her way to achieving her long-term goal of becoming a doctor. "It's not always easy," says Thien, "but I stay motivated by reminding myself that all this hard work will be worth it in the end."

Labeling your goals as short-term or long-term isn't the most important thing you'll need to know about the process. What's more significant is that your goals have the power of the "Three P's." In other words, they're:

1. **Positive!**

   Who could feel fired up about a goal like this, "Stop being such a slob." Or this, "Practice my jump shot, so I don't look like a loser on the court." Be sure to phrase your goals positively to feel good about what you're trying to accomplish. How about, "Clean my room twice a week—and put on some music to make the job more fun." Or, "Practice my jump shot for twenty minutes at least three days this week to improve my skills."

2. **Personal!**

   Remember that your goals must be meaningful to you. They have to reflect your dreams and values. This way, you're guaranteed to feel more motivated to reach them. For example, fourteen-year-old Delfino values nature and loves to be outdoors, so he joined a Scout group. His dream is to become an Eagle Scout, which means he needs to earn a total of twenty-one merit badges. Delfino takes it one badge—one goal—at a time.

3. Possible!

Becoming an ace student or the captain of your team isn't something you can do overnight. When setting goals, it's important to consider what's actually possible. *And* what's within your control. Sometimes people set goals they have little control over, and then feel disappointed about the outcome. For example, suppose you've got a major crush on some guy or girl in your class, and you make it your goal to get that person to like you in the same way. No matter how fascinating you are or how hard you try to win that person over, you may not be able to persuade him or her to like you as more than a friend. Focus on goals that are under your control, so you've got a greater chance of success.

Your goals should also be **"SMART."** What does this mean? The goals you set—whether they're short-term or long-term—need to be:

☑ **S**AVVY

☑ **M**EASURABLE

☑ **A**CTIVE

☑ **R**EACHABLE

☑ **T**IMED

Savvy goals are easy to understand and use. (The opposite are goals that are vague, confusing, or difficult to follow.) To make your goals savvy, keep them specific and within the realm of possibility.

Measurable goals define exactly what you intend to accomplish. Your destination should be crystal clear. To make sure your goals are measurable, get specific about the outcome you want. What do you really hope to achieve?

Active goals tell you what specific *action* you're taking. Active goals include "do it" words, or verbs, that keep you moving forward.

Reachable goals stretch you but still feel within your reach. To check if your goal is reachable, ask yourself, "Do I feel that I can attain this? Is it realistic for me? Is this a challenge I feel comfortable taking?" Your motivation may fizzle if your goal seems unreachable.

Timed goals have clear dates when you'll be able to say, "I did it!" These deadlines give you something to aim for and look forward to. They also motivate you—kind of like school assignment due dates.

What NOT-SO-SMART goals look like:

Goal: "Be a better person."

This is a nice idea, but not a *savvy* goal. Why? Because it's vague. What does "better" mean: kinder, more polite, more organized, stronger? Aiming for a hazy goal like this could leave you feeling confused about your progress.

Goal: "Be the best basketball player on the team."

The problem with this goal is that the measurement (best) is pretty "mushy." How do you measure "best"? Does it mean: scoring the most points, having the highest shot percentage, starting every game, playing more minutes than any other player, getting the most positive press, being named MVP, being selected for the all-conference team, or knowing you tried your hardest? Depending on how you define "best," your strategy for reaching your goal could change dramatically. It's important to have a more clearly *measurable* goal.

Goal: "Feel better about myself."

A worthy aim, but there's no clear "do it" word. What action might you take to feel better? Do you want to eat healthy foods, start a fitness routine, act more confident in social situations, invest in some new clothes, get a different haircut, work harder in school, help someone in your community, or work on your self-image? *Active* goals include strong action words or verbs that help guide you in a positive direction.

Goal: "Get an A+ in chemistry."

Is this goal truly *reachable?* It may be if you're currently in the A range in this class. But what if you're failing chemistry or having a lot of trouble understanding the material? If this is the case, a more reachable goal may be aiming for a C or committing to several tutoring sessions that could help you learn the material you don't understand.

Goal: "Get a new bike next year."

This goal isn't clearly *timed.* Just as you're more likely to work on a school assignment that has a specific due date, you're more likely to work on goals that have clear deadlines. Like your goals themselves, the time frames should be as specific as possible. A deadline like "by May 31, 2002" leaves no doubt as to when you intend to complete your goal.

You can photocopy form #6, "SMART Card," on page 39 and keep it in your Goal Tracker as a reminder to set SMART goals. You can also cut out the card and use it as a bookmark or carry it in your wallet, if you'd like.

THINK IT & INK IT

Have you ever set a NOT-SO-SMART goal? If so, how did you feel about it? What did you learn from the experience? Is there a way you could have revised your goal so that it was SMART? If it's a goal you're still interested in, revise it now and write down three things you could do in the next week to help you move closer to your goal. Use the journal section of your Goal Tracker.

SMART Card

My goals need to be:

SAVVY (easy to understand and use)

MEASURABLE (specific about the outcome)

ACTIVE (clear about the action I need to take)

REACHABLE (within my reach)

TIMED (complete with specific deadlines!)

Goals Come in All Shapes and Sizes

*"A good goal is like a strenuous exercise—
it makes you stretch."—Mary Kay Ash*

The term "one-size-fits-all" hardly ever applies to goals. That's because no two people are alike (and neither are their dreams). What you want may be very different from what your best friend wants—even if the two of you have plenty of other things in common. The way you both approach your goals may vary a lot, too.

Some people aim for lofty long-term goals; others shoot for simple short-term ones. Your goals—whether they're big, small, or somewhere in between—should be the right size for you.

Some Goal Getters find it helpful to divide their goals into categories, such as "School," "Sports," "Friends," and so on. The following categories reflect some SMART goals that teens said were important to them. You may want to use these goals as inspiration for ones you can set in your own life.

Personal

- Learn one new word each day.
- Set up an email account and learn how to use it by the end of the month.
- Play chess at least once each week.
- Read at least one book each quarter.

School

- Improve my grade in math this semester.
- Make the honor roll at least once each year while in high school.
- By the time school starts, find out which West Coast colleges offer degrees in architecture.
- Sign up for the peer tutoring program.

Friends

- Introduce myself to three new people each day.

- Make one new friend each month.

- Compliment at least two friends every day about something other than what they're wearing or how they look.

- When talking to others, say only positive things about my friends who aren't with me right then.

Family

- Call Grandma on the first Sunday of every month.

- Go to the park with my little sister every Wednesday afternoon.

- Willingly say yes to Mom when she asks for help with chores.

- Come home before my curfew when I'm out with my friends.

Community

- Volunteer to serve a meal once a month at a homeless shelter.

- Each quarter, give away the clothes I no longer wear.

- Pick up a piece of litter each day.

- Say "Hi" every day to people I pass on my way to school.

Sports

- Make this year's basketball team.

- Get a personal best in the 100-yard dash during track season.

- Gain five pounds by the time school starts.

- Try out for a sport I didn't play last year.

Work/Money

- By the end of the first week at my new job, make at least one friend who can help me when I have questions.

- Open a checking account by the end of the month.

- Save five hundred dollars this summer for my college fund.

- Each week, donate the price of one school lunch to a food shelf.

Thinking of goals that fall into these categories is a good way to get some perspective on the different areas of your life—including what's working, what needs attention, and what you might change for the better. Here's something to remember, though: You don't have to work on every category at the same time. In fact, you could drive yourself crazy trying to tackle so much at once! No one can consistently improve in every area of life. Overachieving like this is a recipe for stress.

When setting goals for yourself, focus on only one or two major areas at a time. This is plenty. And when pursuing those goals, be sure to leave room for some other essentials in life: sleep, fun, and adventure!

THINK IT & INK IT

Think about the goal categories on pages 40–41 in relation to your own life. Is there one particular category that's stressing you out? If so, why? Are you trying to do too much in that area? Or have you been too busy in other areas to give it a second thought? Come up with at least five ideas for how you might be able to bring that area more in balance. Write your ideas in the journal section of your Goal Tracker.

Here are some words of wisdom from teen Goal Getters:

"When setting goals, the most important thing is to keep your aspirations achievable. It's great to have long-term goals, but I've found it's best to break long-term goals into short-term steps so it feels like you're making progress." ALISON, 19

"I've learned that with perseverance, you can accomplish almost any goal." DREW, 17

"Set a realistic goal for yourself. You should never push yourself over the edge!" JAIMA, 14

"I have lots of goals that are in my control, which feels good. But I also have a goal that's not in my control. I would love to grow taller! But my mom's right when she reminds me to focus on ones I can control." MICHAEL R., 16

"Remember that there are different routes to the same destination or goal, so if things don't seem to be working out, try a new path." REBECCA, 18

"I think the most important thing when setting goals is knowing what you want and realizing it's not going to come to you on a silver platter. You've got to work for it!"
JESSICA, 15

Now it's time to think about what kinds of goals you may want to set for yourself. Pull out your Goal Tracker and look at the pages you've filled out up to this point. In "What Inspires Me?" and "Dream Starters," you wrote about your inspirations, the people you admire, and how you imagine your future. In "Values That Matter to Me," you began to think about the people who mean the most to you in your life and the personal qualities you'd like to have. Then, in "Dare to Dream," you brainstormed what you'd like to accomplish now and in the future. And finally, in your Dreamprint you created a collage of all the things you value and wish for. Here's your chance to start putting all these ideas together.

Based on what you've written in your Goal Tracker so far, ask yourself this big question: What do I *really* want as a goal?

THINK IT & INK IT

In the journal section of your Goal Tracker, write for at least five minutes about the kind of person you want to be and the kind of life you want to live. If you get stuck and can't think of anything, just write "Can't think, can't think" over and over until a new thought breaks through. Ask yourself whether your desires are in line with your values. If they're not, spend a little more time thinking and writing about what you want and why.

If you don't know what you want, figure out what's blocking you. Do you feel that your mom or dad has high expectations of you—and that you have an obligation to meet those expectations (and should put your own wants aside)? Do you doubt that your desires are realistic? Do you think you don't really deserve what you want? Get to the heart of what's preventing you from focusing on what you want. Talking or writing about these feelings is a good way to understand them.

Once you've had time to sort through your feelings, you can start to change your circumstances just the way these teens did:

"I was the goalie on my junior high soccer team, but I decided not to play soccer when I entered high school. I knew high school was going to be harder, and I wanted more time to study. I also wanted to get a part-time job, so I could earn money for college. My teammates gave me a bad time, telling me how much the team needed me and how much they were going to miss me. Even though it meant disappointing my teammates, I chose not to play soccer. Instead I stayed true to myself: I got a job and concentrated on keeping up my grades." AMANDA, 15

"I was going to a high school I didn't really like. I was having a hard time keeping up and so I started skipping classes. I heard about this other high school from a friend, and I really wanted to go to school there instead. I knew it would be a better school for me. My parents agreed. I go there now, and I'm doing much better. I'm getting all A's, and I never skip class." ERIC, 15

"I know more people in my age range who drink alcohol, take drugs, and smoke than people who don't. These people encourage others to do the same. Their suggestions can be tempting, but I'm not interested. Basically, I don't have time to be messing around. There are just too many positive things I want to do." ANIKA, 16

"I really wanted to learn to wrestle but was told by a lot of people that wrestling was for boys. I wouldn't give up, and I finally convinced my family that I was serious. I'm one of only a handful of girls who compete, but I've worked really hard at it. This year, I won the California State Championship for Girls and came in fifth in Greco Roman wrestling, which included both girls and boys. Despite what people said about it being a 'boy's sport,' I knew I could do it." MEGAN, 11

"I've wanted to be a doctor ever since I was a little girl in Vietnam, but I want to make sure I'm doing it for the right reasons. Coming from an Asian family where my parents have a lot of authority and a lot of influence in my life, I have to make sure I'm doing it because it's what I want, not because it's what my parents want." THIEN, 19

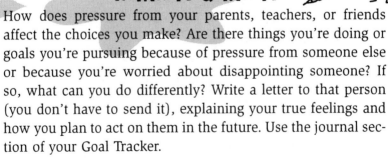

THINK IT & INK IT

How does pressure from your parents, teachers, or friends affect the choices you make? Are there things you're doing or goals you're pursuing because of pressure from someone else or because you're worried about disappointing someone? If so, what can you do differently? Write a letter to that person (you don't have to send it), explaining your true feelings and how you plan to act on them in the future. Use the journal section of your Goal Tracker.

Now do you know what you want to achieve? Once you do, complete form #7, "What I Really Want," on page 47.

What I Really Want

Make a "Top Five List" of what you want—not what others (parents, friends, teachers, the media) seem to want for you. Focus on what's truly meaningful to you. Write your "Top Fives" into sentences that start with the words "I want."

1. _____

_____.

2. _____

_____.

3. _____

_____.

4. _____

_____.

5. _____

_____.

Now choose one of the above as a goal to work on. To put it in the "here and now" (instead of "someday"), rewrite the goal using this sentence starter:

I am working toward _____

_____

_____.

Save the list of "Top Fives" in your Goal Tracker. When you're ready to start a new goal, you can pick another one from the list.

The Goal-Getter Action Plan

"To fail to plan is to plan to fail."—Benjamin Franklin

Goal experts offer lots of different methods for setting goals and achieving success. Which method's the best? No goal-setting process is fool-proof. What works for some people may not work for others. And what works for adults may not always work for teens. For these reasons, I've tried to make the goal-setting process as simple—and fun—as possible. Working on a goal shouldn't be all *work!* There's plenty of room for fun, too.

The most successful action plans are step by step. That's why using a Goal Ladder—complete with rungs that help you take one step at a time—can be a very useful tool. (Plus, ladders help you climb higher, just like goals do!)

Each Goal Ladder you build will be for ONE goal. For example, take a look at your completed "What I Really Want" form. Suppose you wrote, "I am working toward getting to school on time (before 7:30) every day during January." That's your SMART goal, and the Goal Ladder will lead you to it.

Here's how to build a Goal Ladder of your own:

1. **Start with the Goal Ladder form.** Photocopy form #8, "My Goal Ladder," on page 52 and put it in your Goal Tracker. At the top of the form, there's space for you to write your goal. What you want may be a long-term goal or a short-term one. By when do you want to achieve this goal? Set a realistic deadline for yourself and write it in the space provided.

2. **Be sure your Goal Ladder is on solid footing.** Climbing your Goal Ladder is much easier when it's on a strong foundation, which happens when your goals are in line with your values. To double-check yourself, take a look at what you wrote on "Values That Matter to Me" (form #3, pages 20–21). Does the goal you want to work toward seem connected to your values? If not, ask

yourself why you're pursuing this goal . . . is it something you really want? It should be!

3. **Take the "rung-by-rung" approach.** The Goal Ladder is made up of ten "rungs" that help you get from where you are now to the place you want to be. Each rung is basically a way to get closer to the top of the ladder. As you'll see on the "My Goal Ladder" form, there are a total of ten rungs. Ten is a general rule of thumb, not an absolute. You may need more or less than ten, depending on what you plan to accomplish. The three Goal Ladder examples on pages 54–57 will show you ladders of different lengths and how they work.

    What if you know that your goal will definitely need more than ten rungs? Just use the handy "Extension Ladder" (form #9, page 53), which you can photocopy as many times as you'd like.

    > **TIP:** Be sure that your goal isn't so high that there's no end in sight. If you find yourself building a Goal Ladder that's high enough to climb the Empire State Building, take some time to rethink your goal and figure out what you can reasonably achieve.

    If you plan to build a tall (but manageable) ladder, you'll still want to write your goal and deadline in the space provided on your Goal Ladder and on each copy you make of the Extension Ladder. This way, your goal appears on every segment of your ladder—reminding you again and again of what you're reaching for.

4. **Brainstorm.** Brainstorm anything and everything you'll need to do to reach the top of your Goal Ladder by asking yourself what it will take to get from one rung to the next. You can write these ideas on a fresh page of your Goal Tracker. Using the example about getting to school on time, the ideas might include:

    - rise one hour before school begins (6:30 A.M.)

    - get an alarm clock, instead of relying on Dad to wake me

    - practice setting the alarm so I know how to use it

- choose my clothes the night before
- arrange a morning bathroom schedule that the whole family can agree on
- organize my backpack every night
- make lunch the night before
- eat breakfast so I have energy
- be at the bus stop on time

After brainstorming, look over your ideas. Cross out any that don't seem useful, or combine ones that are similar. Now you've got information to put on each rung of your Goal Ladder.

5. **Work your way up from the bottom of the ladder.** Number the remaining ideas or rewrite them in an order that seems logical. To do this, think about what action you need to take first. (Your first rung represents the first thing you need to do to get started.) In the school example, it makes sense to get an alarm clock and learn to set it. What comes next? And what comes after that? It's really up to you. There are no right or wrong answers when making a Goal Ladder—just put the ideas in an order that works for you. Now count them: How many do you have? Less than ten? More than ten? Check out the sample Goal Ladders on pages 54–57. Using them as a guide, arrange your ideas rung by rung on your own Goal Ladder. When you're done, you should have a great visual record of each step you'll take!

6. **Set your deadlines.** How long will each action take to complete, and by when do you want to complete it? Keep in mind how many other things you and your family may have going on. (Pull out your calendar or daily planner, test schedule, or game schedule, so you can make sure you're not assigning deadlines that conflict with other activities.) Set deadlines that are manageable—not too far ahead, but not so tight that you feel squeezed by them. Now write them on each rung, along with the action you'll take.

TIP: Some rungs may have a deadline like "Every day," or "Each night," or "After school every Monday." That's fine, as long as these expectations are reasonable.

7. **Seal the deal.** Once you've filled in your Goal Ladder, sign your name. This "contract" with yourself tells you that you're serious about completing your goal.

8. **Spread the word.** You may want to show your finished Goal Ladder to your family and friends, so they know what you're setting out to accomplish. To stay motivated, you can display extra copies of your finished Goal Ladder in your locker, in your backpack, on your bulletin board, or anyplace else where you'll see it often.

The great thing about the Goal Ladder is that if you keep climbing rung by rung, you'll eventually reach your destination. And just like climbing a real ladder, the more you do it, the easier it gets!

THINK IT & INK IT

Imagine you've just climbed to the top of your Goal Ladder. You open the most recent issue of your school or community paper and see an article about you and what you've accomplished. In the journal section of your Goal Tracker, write the article (it can be short!) as you'd like to see it. Explain your goal, what steps you took to reach it, why it was important to you, and how you feel now that you've achieved it.

My Goal Ladder

Photocopy for your
Goal Tracker!!!

My goal:_____

_____

My deadline:_____

_____

Sign here:

_____

_____

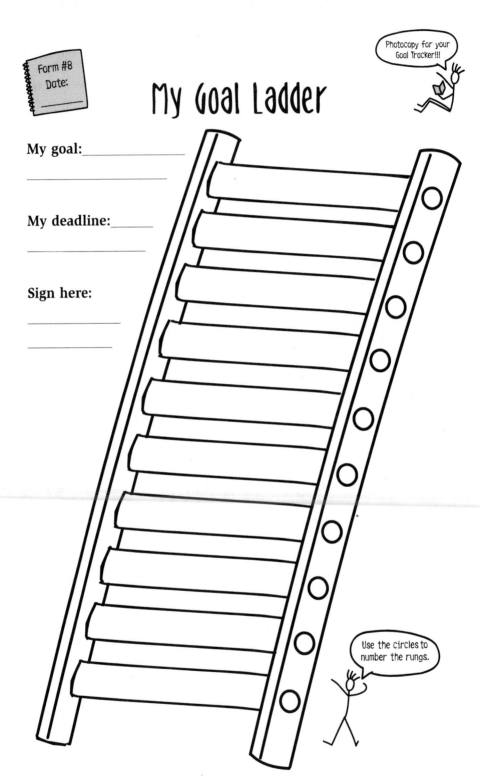

Use the circles to
number the rungs.

Form #9
Date:_____

Extension Ladder

Photocopy for your Goal Tracker!!!

My goal:_____

_____

My deadline:_____

_____

Sign here:

_____

_____

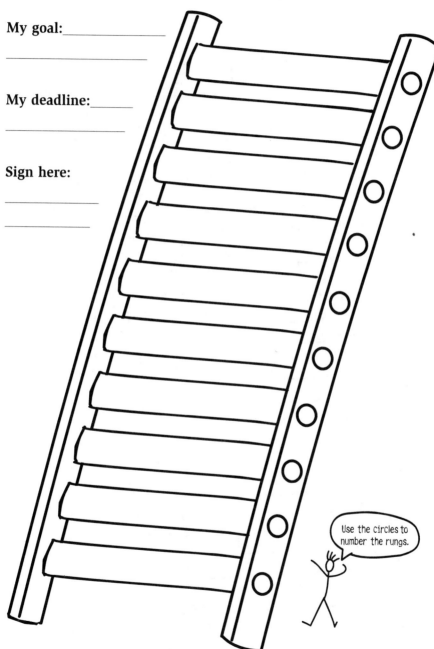

Use the circles to number the rungs.

What Goal Ladders can look like:

My goal: Get a part-time job after school.

My deadline: By Nov. 15

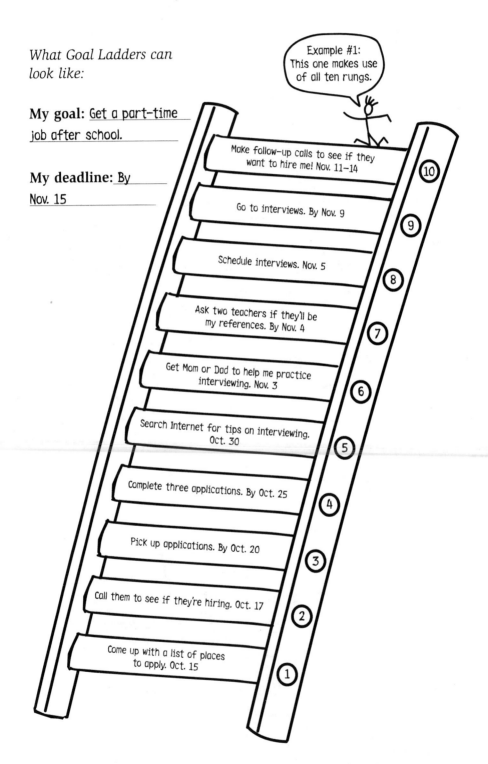

Example #1:
This one makes use of all ten rungs.

Make follow-up calls to see if they want to hire me! Nov. 11–14 ⑩

Go to interviews. By Nov. 9 ⑨

Schedule interviews. Nov. 5 ⑧

Ask two teachers if they'll be my references. By Nov. 4 ⑦

Get Mom or Dad to help me practice interviewing. Nov. 3 ⑥

Search Internet for tips on interviewing. Oct. 30 ⑤

Complete three applications. By Oct. 25 ④

Pick up applications. By Oct. 20 ③

Call them to see if they're hiring. Oct. 17 ②

Come up with a list of places to apply. Oct. 15 ①

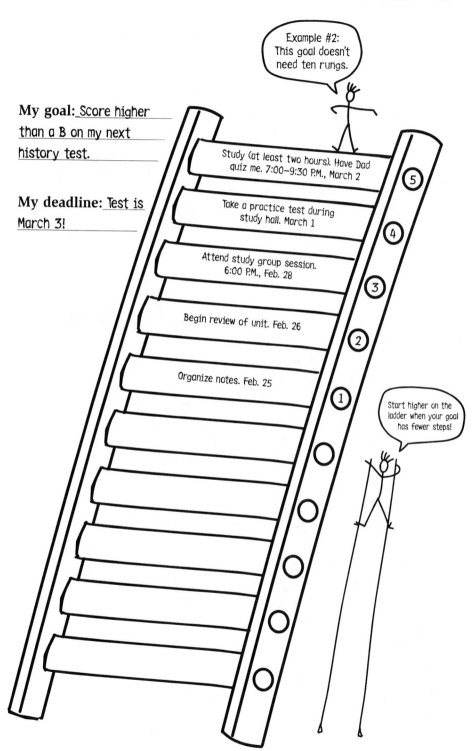

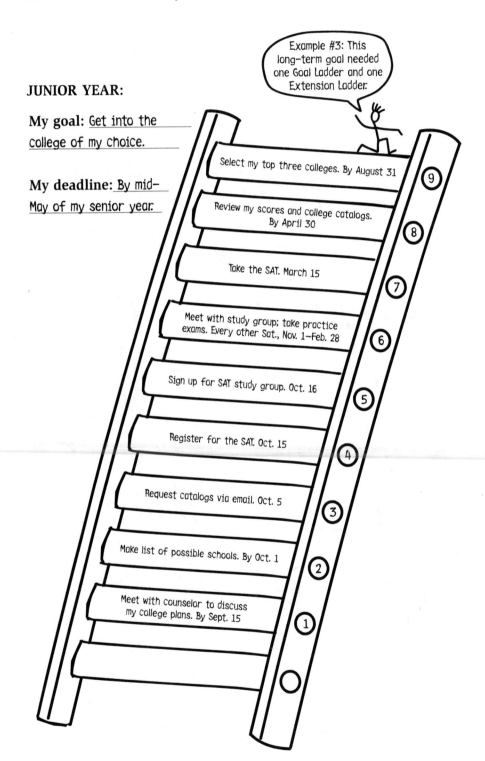

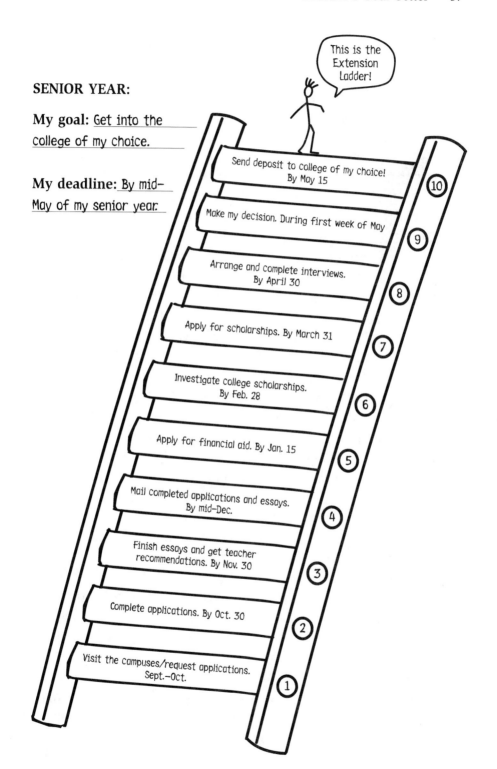

GOAL GETTERS IN ACTION

MAX, from Barrington, Illinois, was eleven when he heard that an inner-city school in Chicago was in bad need of sports equipment. Max attended a school that had plenty of equipment to use during recess, and he thought it would be a good idea to give kids at another school the same.

"When I first heard about the school, I asked my mom if we could buy them a basketball hoop and a few balls," says Max. "She said 'Great idea,' and then asked me how I planned to come up with the money. Without thinking about it, I said I'd have a fund-raiser. I knew I could raise money that way because I'd seen my mom do it. After brainstorming ideas, I decided on selling pizzas. My mom had just bought a make-your-own pizza kit from someone who was raising money for the high school swim team. I thought the pizza was pretty good and figured other kids would think so, too."

Max knew he wouldn't be able to sell enough pizzas on his own, so his next step was to get his teammates and classmates involved. With the help of his basketball coach, he wrote a letter to all the other kids in his school, explaining his goal, asking if they'd be willing to help sell pizzas, and inviting them to a taste-test at recess, so they could try the pizzas for themselves. "I figured other kids would be more willing to help if they knew how good the pizzas tasted," says Max. "Besides, free food is a great incentive."

During the taste-test, Max explained to his classmates why he needed their help and presented his action plan, which included a schedule detailing when orders were due, when pizzas would be ready to be picked up, and when the money had to be turned in. With the help of more than one hundred classmates, Max raised enough money to buy sports equipment for the school as well as a storage shed for when it wasn't being used. Thanks to his action plan (and the help of others), he achieved his goal—and a whole lot more.

Form #10
Date:

Conversation Starters

Photocopy for your Goal Tracker!!!

Ask these questions of friends, family members, or other people in your life.

- How do you decide what steps to take to reach your goals? And how do you keep track of these steps?

- How do you balance the goals that you'll reach in the next month with ones that will take years to achieve?

- Do you like to have lots of goals at once, or do you focus on one major goal at a time?

- What general advice do you have about setting goals and reaching them?

- What's the biggest goal you've ever reached? What was the key to your success?

Get "Goaling"

> "Without goals and plans to reach them,
> you are like a ship that has set sail
> with no destination."—Fitzhugh Dodson

By giving you something to work toward, goals provide a sense of direction. They help you feel like you're going somewhere in life. When you plan out a goal, you take control of your future. And each step you take gets you closer to your dreams. Are you ready to set up your own Goal Ladder? How about doing it TODAY!?

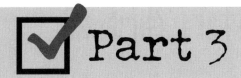

Part 3

PUT IT ALL TOGETHER

Start Climbing!

> "You don't have to be great to get going, but you have to get going to be great."—Les Brown

If you've got your Goal Ladder (see pages 48–57) in place, you're ready to go. You can begin climbing the rungs any time. In fact, now is as good a time as any! Why not get started right this moment? Part 3 is all about getting going and staying on track. You'll learn lots of techniques that Goal Getters use to focus and to keep moving forward.

But what if you don't feel quite ready to start yet? What if you've been telling yourself, "I'll do it later" or "I'll start tomorrow"? Putting your goals off—otherwise known as procrastinating—is an obstacle you just might face.

If you're procrastinating, you have plenty of company. Everyone does it at one time or another, but if you find yourself in the trap of making endless excuses, ask yourself why. Are you . . .

- unsure about how to take the first step?

- worried about failure?

- convinced you don't have enough time to do a good job?

- anxious about succeeding?

- waiting for the "perfect" time to produce "perfect" results?

Remember that the longer you procrastinate, the less motivated you'll probably become. You may even put off your goal (and the dream it supports) for so long that you forget about it altogether. That can lead to feelings of guilt.

THINK IT & INK IT

If you're having trouble getting started on your goal, open the journal section of your Goal Tracker and write a list of all the reasons why you can't pursue your goal. Write down all your negative thoughts and your fears, no matter how big or small they are. Now, tear out the list and throw it away. Tell yourself you're not going to let your thoughts and fears get in the way of your goal.

Here are some tried-and-true tips to help you blast through procrastination barriers:

1. **Take ten.** Tell yourself you'll spend just ten minutes on your goal. This small effort will usually be enough to break through your resistance.

2. **Use the time and resources that are available.** Don't wait until you have an entire evening to begin working toward your goal. Get started, even if you have only twenty minutes to spare. In that little amount of time, you can accomplish something small—and one small accomplishment can be a great motivator.

3. **Give yourself a reward.** Tell yourself that after taking one step or meeting a deadline successfully, you'll give yourself a reward. A reward can be that extra incentive you need to feel motivated.

4. **Set "Anti Deadlines."** This is the opposite of rewards. You might tell yourself, "If I don't do it by 9 P.M., I can't visit my favorite Web site."

5. **Recruit a "get-up-and-go" coach.** Ask a friend, classmate, teacher, parent, or someone else you trust to help you get moving.

6. **Make time.** Are you overcommitted to lots of other activities—sports, clubs, service projects, social events, and so on? Do you enjoy all of these activities equally, or would you be willing to give one up so you have more time to concentrate on your goal? Do you waste several hours a day watching TV, surfing the Internet, or talking on the phone? Consider cutting down on these time-wasters, so you can focus on your goal.

Need some advice on managing your time?

- **Get a calendar or daily planner to carry with you.** These tools help you see your days, weeks, and months at a glance. You can keep a record of your test dates, school assignments, appointments, scheduled events, activities—and, of course, your Goal Ladder deadlines. Once you start using a calendar or daily planner, you'll probably find (as many Goal Getters have) that writing things down encourages you to better plan your days.

- **Make to-do lists.** You can create these lists for each day or each week, depending on your preference. You may want to organize your lists into categories like "School," "Goals," "At Home," etc., or you may just want to have one BIG list that includes everything. Start listing your tasks, and then rank them in order of importance. (Be sure that your goals are a  high priority!) Now put the high-priority items at the top of the list, so you always tackle them first. Cross off each job you complete. If you want, make a new list of the things you still have to do, so you don't lose track.

"The best I can tell you is get a planner and write down when and where all your activities are. Plan ahead for rides and other stuff you'll need. Write down in the daily portion of your planner all the things you have to do, even if you know you won't get them all done that day: your homework, taking out the trash, your English paper, practicing SAT sample questions, or whatever. And don't forget more personal things like exercising and calling a friend. I even have to write down deep-cleaning my face or I'll forget." ANIKA, 16

"I generally plan my schedule for the week on Sunday night. I look at everything I need to get done and all the places I need to be, and I try to come up with a schedule for the week that keeps my life in balance." PETTUS, 18

The Power of Positive Thoughts and Words

"You've got to believe in yourself. The more you love and accept yourself, the sooner you'll be able to reach your goals."—Florence Griffith Joyner

Keeping yourself motivated, enthusiastic, and flexible are daily deeds of daring when you're going after your goals. There are days when you won't need that extra boost—you'll wake up full of energy and ready to do whatever it takes. But on some days, you may need to find ways to charge yourself up. What can you do? Jump-start your confidence!

When your confidence is high, you're more able to make good decisions and take action. When it's not, even the smallest tasks can become difficult. You probably already know that the better you feel about yourself, the more successful you'll be—in school and in life.

Need some confidence boosters? Use a new page in your Goal Tracker to try one or all of the following activities:

1. **List your good qualities.** List what you like about yourself and what other people like about you. Read the list once a day.

2. **Appreciate what you have.** Make a list of the big and small things you're thankful for. Review the list whenever you're feeling down or unsure. By focusing on what you have, rather

than on what you don't have, you'll fill your day with a sense of appreciation.

3. **Do one thing today that you consider healthy.** You'll send yourself a message that you're worth taking care of, even if you don't feel so great about yourself at the moment. Use your Goal Tracker to record what you plan to do and how you felt after doing it.

4. **Remember compliments.** Recall some of the best compliments you've ever received and write them all down. (And the next time someone says something nice about you, be sure to believe it! Accept praise with a smile.)

5. **Let go of worries.** Instead of letting your mind run in circles, write down any thoughts or worries that are bothering you. When you see them on paper, they won't seem so big anymore—and you may just find a solution as you're writing. If not, talk to someone you trust about what's going on.

6. **Do something nice for someone else.** Pick up a piece of trash, wash the dishes (without being asked), do some volunteer work, or help a friend with a problem. Write about how this felt for you.

Sometimes people forget to recognize their own talents and good qualities. Get a reality check on your strong suits by getting together with three or four friends in a quiet, comfortable place. Make a copy of form #11, "What Others See in Me," on page 68 for each person in the group. One by one, tell each person what you like about him or her: the strengths and positive qualities you see, the ways this friend makes you feel good, admirable things he or she has done. Be sincere and say only the things you really mean. When it's your turn to listen to others, use your form to write down everything you hear. Try not to comment, disagree, or act surprised. Just write. Or, if you prefer, you can pass your forms around the circle, writing your comments about each other. Keep your finished form in your Goal Tracker. Then, whenever you're feeling less than confident, go back and look at all the kind things people have said about you. You'll feel better, and you might even discover great parts of yourself you hadn't been aware of before.

"I have a poster in my closet that my friends from camp signed. I look at it whenever I'm feeling down and need a 'lift-up.' They all wrote really nice things about me, and it makes me feel so much better to know how much I'm appreciated." JULIA M., 14

"I keep cards from my friends on a shelf in my room. Whenever I see them, I'm reminded of how many people care about me." MEGHAN, 15

"I try to remember the nice things people say about me, particularly when I'm having a bad day or am worried that I might not do well at something. Remembering that others believe in me helps me believe in myself." MICHAEL R., 16

THINK IT & INK IT

Learning to recognize your own strengths and good qualities is important. Write a letter to yourself, acknowledging all your positive traits. Try to include at least ten things that you really like about yourself and the reasons why. Then, when you need a lift, you can use the letter as a reminder of how capable you really are. Use the journal section of your Goal Tracker.

What Others See in Me

Use the spaces below to fill in all the nice things others say about you.

Many teens, even those who are positive on the outside and seem to have everything going for them, are occasionally plagued by negative thoughts: *I'm not good enough. I never succeed in anything. What's the point in trying?* You might sometimes have thoughts like this yourself. That voice inside your head is kind of like the anchorperson on the news, providing a running commentary about everything that's going on in your life. Most people aren't aware that these internal conversations are very influential. Suppose the voice—also known as your "inner critic"—is generally grouchy? When this is the case, your mind is filled with negative thoughts, which drain your energy. On the other hand, if the voice in your head tends to be positive and cheery, you feel a whole lot better about yourself. That's the power of positive thinking!

The next time you hear your inner critic complaining, tell yourself you're not going to listen to what it has to say. Think of this process as tuning out your negative thoughts and tuning in to positive ones. Here's how it works:

Tune out:	Tune in to:
"I'm so stupid."	"I'm great at ____ (fill in the blank)."
"I'm really bad at this."	"I'll do better next time."
"I really blew it today."	"A mistake isn't the end of the world."
"There's no point to this. I'll just fail."	"I'm going to give it a try."
"I can't do anything right."	"I can't expect myself to be perfect. No one is."
"I'd better do it right or I'll quit."	"I'll give it my best!"

If you want to have a more positive outlook overall, get in the habit of looking at every part of your life and seeing the good rather than the bad. *Attitude*—not talent, money, or popularity—plays a bigger role than you may imagine in determining your future success. If you believe that you'll succeed, you'll put yourself in a problem-solving, goal-setting frame of mind that will more easily take you through the rough spots and put you in the fast lane to your dreams.

To keep your attitude positive, you can:

- **Cheer yourself on (inside your head).** "Way to go!" or "I can do it!" may be just what you need to hear to stay motivated and feeling good.

- **Let it go.** If you make a mistake at some point (and everyone does), apologize if you need to and move on. Dwelling on your errors won't get you anywhere. Letting them go helps you keep moving in a positive direction.

- **Reward yourself.** Keep track of your efforts to change your attitude. Use your Goal Tracker to record any negative thoughts and the positive ones you've replaced them with. When you've successfully converted ten downer thoughts into positive views, reward yourself with something that's meaningful to you.

Affirmations are another way to focus on the positive. To affirm means to "make firm" whatever you dream or imagine. By writing and saying your affirmations over and over, you can replace the self-defeating thoughts of your inner critic with the voice of your inner champion.

Here are some examples:

"I'm really creative."

"I'm true to myself."

"I'm strong and physically fit."

"I can make a difference."

"I can inspire others to make a difference."

"I can do whatever I put my mind to."

Here are a few tips to make your affirmations as powerful as possible:

- **Stay in the present.** Phrase your affirmations in the present tense, not future tense. (If you phrase your affirmations in the future, you'll always be waiting for the results to happen.) For example, keep telling yourself, "I am pursuing my goals," rather than "I will pursue my goals."

- **Keep it positive.** Phrase affirmations in the most positive way you can. Affirm what you do want, not what you *don't* want. Say "I wake up early every morning feeling full of energy," instead of "I won't oversleep anymore."

- **Be specific.** Like goals, affirmations are most effective when they're specific. For instance, "I'm working with people I really like in a job I value" is better than "I've got a job for the summer."

- **Keep it simple**. Make sure your affirmations are short and focused on one idea.

Using the tips you just read, write two or three affirmations in support of your goals. Once you're happy with your affirmations, record them on a new page in your Goal Tracker. (You can also write them on index cards or bright paper, putting them in places where you'll see them several times each day—on a mirror, near your bed, inside your wallet, in your locker, or as a screensaver on your computer.) Then begin putting your affirmations to work. Read them out loud until you know them by heart. Say the words as if you really mean them. Think about them and feel their power. You can say your affirmations to yourself, either silently or out loud, several times each day. Say them while you comb your hair, on the way to school, during your workout, or while you're setting the table. The more you use them, the more effective they'll become.

You can record affirmations on a cassette tape and then listen to them. Affirmations can also be sung to any song—a catchy, familiar tune works well. Start with a song you know, and then make up new words that tell the story of who you want to be. Then sing it—and move your body when you do. Sing it while you're in the shower, cruising the mall, or watching TV. The more often you repeat your song—and the more involved you get when you do—the more you'll plant your dream deep in your mind where success will grow.

"My favorite affirmation is this: 'I am completely independent in every way. I, and I alone, have the power to make every decision that affects my life.' It keeps me going!" EMILY, 18

If you're having trouble coming up with your own affirmations or if you want a few extras, use form #12, "Words To-Go," on page 73. You can photocopy the page, cut out the affirmations you like best, and carry them with you. Repeat these positive sayings often. You can even have them laminated at a copy center, if you'd like.

THINK IT & INK IT

Writing affirmations over and over is another way of planting their positive messages in your mind. In the journaling section of your Goal Tracker, write each of your affirmations ten times, each time tuning in to the power of the words. You can write the affirmations each morning when you get up, during the day when you have a few quiet minutes, or every night before bed.

Form #12
Date:
_____

Photocopy for your
Goal Tracker!!!

Words To-Go

I take care of myself, inside and out, every day.	I keep moving toward my goals, step by step.
I'm getting stronger every day in every way.	I trust myself to make the right decisions.
I ask for help when I need it.	I'm a positive thinker.
I'm capable of setting and reaching SMART goals.	What I need is within my reach.

Visualize Your Success

"You must first visualize yourself as a success in order to be a success."—Rosa Diaz

Visualization is another tool that harnesses the power of your imagination. There's nothing complicated about it. In fact, you already know how to visualize. You do it every time you daydream: imagining yourself as the first runner to cross the finish line, seeing your teacher hand you a paper with an A on it, picturing yourself starting your own business. These are all examples of visualization and how you use imagination to help create your future. It's like having your own private movie with the ending in your hands.

If you're an athlete, you may have already practiced visualization. You've probably heard or read about amateurs, professionals, and Olympic athletes who imagine themselves flawlessly executing their moves, calmly and without fear. Skaters practice every jump and turn while lying in bed, skiers boldly slalom down the mountainside while taking a walk around the block, and golfers play entire rounds in their mind while eating breakfast.

Think about your goal. Is there a particular moment that sums up everything you want about it? Visualize the scene, imagining new details every time you roll the image through your mind. Think about the sights, sounds, smells, feelings, and anything else that can help make the image of your success more real. Hear the applause for your first dramatic performance, feel the weight of the trophy in your hands, smell the saltwater as you picture putting on your scuba gear . . .

Your mind produces what it dwells on. If you focus on disappointment or failure, be prepared to experience less than what you really could. Always visualize the *positive*. See yourself winning the race, not tripping over your feet as you leave the starting blocks. See yourself getting applause when you finish your speech, not blanking out in front of the entire class. See yourself reaching your goal with ease, and you're far more likely to succeed.

The more often you visualize your success, the more motivated you'll feel. Visualize at the beginning of the day, when you first wake up. Visualize as you're falling asleep at night or when you're getting a ride to practice. Picture yourself doing well—in the classroom, on a race course, in social situations, or while raising money for a cause you believe in. Let yourself feel how it will be to have that success.

Not sure how to visualize? Here's how in seven easy steps:

1. Find a comfortable position, either lying down or sitting in a quiet place where you won't be disturbed. Relax. Take three deep breaths all the way down into your abdomen. With each inhale, say *I am*. With each exhale, say *relaxed.* As you exhale, let your muscles go limp. Beginning with your toes and moving up to your scalp, let your muscles relax.

2. Let any negative thoughts and self-doubt break free. Feel them leave your body each time you exhale. See them floating away, clearing your mind to focus on your goal.

3. Imagine your Goal Ladder and the final goal you'd like to reach. Set this image firmly in your mind.

4. Now imagine yourself reaching this goal. If it's an event, picture yourself there. What are you wearing? Who's with you? If it's an object, feel it in your hands and imagine showing it to your friends. If it's a task, see yourself smoothly working on it. If it's a situation, see yourself there exactly as you'd like to be, feeling self-confident, capable, and in control.

5. Keep adding details until you can see the finished goal fully in your mind. See, hear, smell, taste, and touch your goal as if it were actually happening. Take five minutes to see yourself fully enjoying and appreciating what you've reached for.

6. Keeping the image firmly in mind, repeat an affirmation such as, "Here I am, doing exactly what I want to do," or "It feels so great to be finished with that project," or "I am happy with myself in this situation."

7. Now keep that vision of success with you as you climb the rungs of your Goal Ladder. The image will help you stay motivated every step of the way!

Here are some other ways to visualize your success:

- **Believe it.** If you believe you're a Goal Getter, you'll start acting like one.

- **Fake it.** If you act a certain way long enough, it becomes a part of you. If you walk and talk with confidence, stand erect, and take deep, relaxing breaths, guess what? You'll feel more confident. Try it!

- **Create it.** Suppose your goal is to make your high school soccer team. Copy the team picture from last year's yearbook, and put a picture of yourself in the photo. Hang the photo where you'll see it often. Or, if you want to write and perform your own songs, draw a cover for your future best-selling CD, put it in a jewel case, and display it near your family's stereo or boombox.

- **Try it on for size.** Just like you'd try on a new pair of shoes before buying them, you can try on parts of your goal for size, too. For example, make your own business cards and see how your name looks with a title like "Yearbook Editor" after it.

GOAL GETTERS IN ACTION

Thirteen-year-old **TOMMY** loves to fish and is out on the water most summer days. "Before I go to sleep at night, I picture myself pulling in a nine-pound walleye," he says. "When my alarm goes off in the morning, even though it's still dark, I'm really motivated to get out of bed and get onto the lake as fast as I can. I even visualize what it will be like when I'm a professional fisherman: the mist on the water, the jacket I'll wear, and the boat I'll have."

Seventeen-year-old **JOYCE** wants a better relationship with her mom. They used to get along pretty well, but lately they've been arguing about Joyce's boyfriend. "I really respect my mom and want to get along with her, but it's not always easy," says Joyce. "I picture the two of us having a pleasant, five-minute conversation. I actually see myself sit down to dinner with her, feel myself smiling, and see her do the same. This seems to help."

MICHAEL S., also seventeen, wants to be a sports broadcaster. "I practice in my mind all the time," he says. "Even when I'm watching a game with my friends, I keep my own running commentary going in my head. In fact, I picture myself sitting next to Dick Vitale or Bob Costas. I even hear them say, 'Michael, what do you think just happened there?' or 'Now, down to Michael, who's in the locker room with the winning quarterback.' Stuff like this keeps me really motivated and helps me believe in myself."

Eighteen-year-old **REBECCA** gives speeches in support of her volunteer work. The night before delivering a big speech, she imagines herself confidently walking to the front of the auditorium, pulling out her notes, and flawlessly delivering her speech. She sees her audience paying attention to what she's saying, nodding in agreement, and applauding enthusiastically. "By practicing in my mind ahead of time, I feel much more confident when I'm in front of a roomful of people."

Get Some Support

"It's always more meaningful and wonderful when you can share your goals and your life with others. Great friends and family are key."—Missy Giove

The help and support of other people is another key to reaching your goals. Friends, family, teachers, guidance counselors, coaches, neighbors, members of the community, and even people you haven't met yet have the skills and inspiration you may need. One of the first ways to get support for your efforts is to share your goals with your friends and family. Have you shown them your Goal Ladder yet?

There are three basic types of help most people need to keep moving toward a goal: get-there help, know-how help, and feel-good help.

Get-there help is the practical stuff you need to complete your Goal Ladder. For example:

- a ride to and from meetings or practices
- money for supplies or lessons
- a chaperone to escort you on an out-of-town trip
- directions to a place you've never been
- help building or making something
- access to equipment you need
- advice about how to resolve a problem
- a proofreader to review your application

Get-there help often comes from family members, friends, and other people you already know. It may also come from your school or a service organization, depending on what you need. The people around you can offer the resources you're seeking—but only if you're willing to ask. Show them your Goal Ladder and explain what you're aiming to achieve. They'll see you're willing to do your part to make your goal happen, and they'll know a little help can go a long way.

TIP: When you share your goals, you may discover that other people have the same interests as you and could use your support in turn. Ask your friends what you can do to help them, and tell them how they can help you. This might be as simple as reminding each other to stay on schedule or congratulating each other on small achievements.

Know-how help teaches you what you need to know to reach your goal. Maybe you've heard yourself saying, "I'd like to do that, but I don't know how" or "I'd start on my goal, but I don't know what to do." You're not alone. In fact, almost everyone has thoughts like this, particularly when starting something new. Instead of using these thoughts as an excuse to give up, you can figure out a way to learn what you need to know.

You probably already do this on a regular basis. Whenever you ask someone to explain a math problem or show you a new skateboard trick, you're getting someone with know-how to teach you what you want to learn. You can do the same thing for your goals. What do you need to know to keep moving up your Goal Ladder? Check the library or the Internet for answers. Talk to your parents or teachers. Ask a friend. Or look for programs or classes geared toward teens in your area. Your community center or school guidance counselor can be a resource, too. Do whatever it takes to keep going for your goals!

Feel-good help is for those inevitable days when, no matter how hard you try, it's almost impossible to feel good about what you're doing. You may be cruising along, enjoying a great week, only to be brought up short by "one of those days." You wake up late, get into an argument with your best friend, make a mental error that costs your team a run, show up late for dinner, or realize as you crawl into bed that you didn't think about your Goal Ladder once the entire day. That's when you need feel-good help (and it doesn't hurt to have it at other times as well).

A hug from your mom or dad, a compliment from a teacher, or a "Great job!" from a friend are all things that can help you feel good about yourself. Feel-good help can inspire you, motivate you, or bring you up on a down day. And feel-good help can come from anywhere: family members who love you unconditionally, caring friends who know how to listen, coaches who motivate you to keep trying even though you think you stink, teachers who build your confidence, and that special someone who keeps you on the right path when you're struggling. If you're not getting the feel-good help you need, *ask for it* from people who care about you.

 ## GOAL GETTERS IN ACTION

How do other teens use get-there help? Sixteen-year-old **ANIKA** says, "This summer, I'm going backpacking for a month in Montana. It's a big expense. I've been working at a bakery in my neighborhood to earn some of the money. My parents are going to pay the rest." **AMANDA,** fifteen, says, "My parents always drive me to and from work. If they weren't willing to do that, I wouldn't be able to keep my job."

How about know-how help? Sixteen-year-old **MELISSA** says, "I've learned a lot of stuff from Mark, a counselor at my school who teaches Life Skills. He helped me learn how to study and budget my money. Thanks to him, I'm getting better grades and I've already saved two thousand dollars this year, so I can buy a better car before I start college." **TOMMY,** thirteen, says, "John, who used to be my next-door neighbor and now lives a few miles away, has taught me a lot about fishing: how to read a lake, what to do when the fish aren't biting, and how to fillet the fish I catch."

Feel-good help makes a difference in these teens' lives: Fifteen-year-old **ERIC** says, "I work at a grocery store. Even though my job's not all that glamorous, the people I work with make me feel it's really important and that what I do matters." **LYNDZEY,** age sixteen, says, "My cousin is always there for me. He really listens to me, and that helps me sort out my problems." Twelve-year-old **MATT** says, "I play a lot of sports. My coaches are all really good at motivating me. Sometimes it's a pat on the back, sometimes it's a smile, sometimes it's a pre-game pep talk. Even though I'm not always the best player, they make me feel important."

Want to know about someone who can provide get-there help, know-how help, *and* feel-good help? That person is known as a mentor—a wise, trusted guide who meets with you on a regular basis to help you reach your goals. Just as a master shares experience and knowledge with an apprentice, a mentor invests time and skills to help you develop your dreams and get what you really want. A mentor can help you stay on track as a Goal Getter, introduce you to other successful people, boost your confidence, and more.

Your mentor can be someone you know (a friend of your mom's or dad's) or someone you don't know (the owner of a local business). Many organizations—including Big Brothers Big Sisters of America, the YMCA, and the YWCA—bring teens and mentors together. You'll find listings for these organizations in the Goal-Getter Resources on pages 117–124.

How do you hook up with a mentor on your own? Approaching a would-be mentor can seem intimidating, especially if you don't know the person well but have admired him or her from afar. Remember that this person probably had a mentor along the way and, as a result, may be willing to mentor you. But you'll never know until you ask.

If you've never met the person you want as a mentor, you'll have to introduce yourself and convince the person to help you. You can introduce yourself in person, make a phone call, write a letter, or send an email message. Include the following information:

- your name and contact information

- the name of the person, if any, who recommended you

- your goal and why you'd like to have a mentor

- what specific help you'd like from your mentor

- why you think the person you've selected would be a good mentor

- when you'd first like to meet and how often after that

- a thank you

Before you call your would-be mentor on the phone or talk in person, think about what you'd like to say. Just as actors rehearse their lines before a performance, you may want to practice your end of the conversation a few times so you feel more confident. If he or she says no, thank the person anyway and ask if he or she could suggest someone else who would make a good mentor for you. Then make the next call right away, so you keep your momentum. It's natural to feel discouraged when you hear no, but with persistence, you'll eventually get a yes from someone else.

Once you have a mentor, you'll want to make the most of your time with that person. These tips can help:

1. Be willing and eager to learn.

2. Have a list of specific questions or topics you want to discuss.

3. Take notes in your Goal Tracker.

4. When your mentor asks you a question, avoid giving a one-word answer. Get into the habit of being open and talkative.

5. Always say thanks and let your mentor know how much you appreciate the help.

As with every other part of goal setting, asking for help and support gets easier the more you do it. Track down anyone and everyone who can help you reach your goals. You'll be surprised to find out how many people are experts in one thing or another—and how willing they are to help. Behind every great achiever is a group of friends, classmates, advisors, and supporters who have helped along the way.

No matter what the outcome of the help you get, say thanks to the people who have given their time and expertise. Thank yous are simple, important, and often overlooked. Next time you go to a movie, look at the credits. Or note the acknowledgments listed in the front or back of a book you're reading. Or check out the liner notes in a CD case. You'll find that filmmakers, authors, and musicians say thanks to all sorts of people. "Thank you" only takes a second to say or write, but it might just make someone's day.

GOAL GETTERS IN ACTION

DREW, age seventeen, has a mentor named Fran, one of his teachers and the advisor to his high school Outreach Club. "When my classmates and I were trying to figure out how we could help address the issue of hunger in our community, Fran helped us develop an action plan and kept us focused on our goal."

Thirteen-year-old **CARLY'S** mentor is her aunt. "For years, she's been a world-class log roller, one of the events in the Lumberjack World Championships each summer in Hayward, Wisconsin. She's teaching me how to improve my technique and how to mentally hold my own with the older girls I compete against."

Sixteen-year-old **ANIKA'S** mentor is a teacher at the Children's Theatre where she takes classes. "I've been studying with him for two years, and I've grown so much as an actor because of him. He knows how to push me to do my best and when to let me be so I don't get too discouraged. He's given me opportunities that I might not have had otherwise, such as a chance to watch rehearsals of plays he's working on."

Fourteen-year-old **DELFINO'S** mentor, Mike, acts as his personal trainer: "He's got a black belt in karate and has taught me everything he knows. This summer he's going to teach me how to lift weights because I really want to make the high school football team."

PATTI, age sixteen, says, "I want to be an artist and have learned a lot about art from my mentor, LeeAnne. She's now going to art school in New York City, but whenever she's home, she takes me to an exhibition, teaches me something new, and helps me work on my own technique. She encourages me to follow my dreams, no matter how fantastic they may seem."

Need some help yourself? On page 85, is form #13, called "Help I Need." You can photocopy it for your Goal Tracker and use it as you climb each of the rungs of your Goal Ladder.

For every step you plan to take, ask yourself, "What help do I need to accomplish this?" Write it down on the form, and be as specific as you can. If you need money, *how much* money? Do you need help learning a new skill? *Which* skill? A confidence boost? *When* would it mean the most to you? Think of all the ways someone might be able to assist you. Don't worry about where the help is going to come from just yet. For now, concentrate on creating a complete list of the get-there, know-how, and feel-good help you need as you climb your Goal Ladder.

Now that you've identified what you need, it's time to consider who might be able to help you. Think about the most knowledgeable people you know (your friends as well as adults), and even people you may be acquainted with but don't know well (such as teachers you've never had before, your principal). Once you've created a list of people who might be able to help with the specific rungs of your Goal Ladder, fill in the right-hand column of form #13 with their names and contact information (phone numbers, office hours, etc.). Whenever possible, write down more than one person, so you'll have a backup option if your first choice doesn't work out.

Ready to ask for help? If it's someone you know, get on the phone or visit in person and ask for what you need. If it's someone you don't know, introduce yourself and talk about what you're looking for. When you do connect with someone who can help, be sure to show him or her your Goal Ladder. Here are some things you'll want to explain to your would-be helper:

- your goal

- what kind of help you'll need

- when you'll need it

- how much time you think it will take to help you

After you've sought out the help you need, congratulate yourself on a job well done. Now you can keep climbing your Goal Ladder rung by rung.

Photocopy for your
Goal Tracker!!!

Help I Need

My Goal:_____

_____

What I need help with:	Who can help:

form a Dream Team

> "No matter what accomplishments you achieve, somebody helps you."—Althea Gibson

After you've found a handful of people who are willing and able to help, you may even want to form your own personal Dream Team. Your Dream Team can be made up of a few trusted people who are as committed to your success as you are. Whenever you need help—whether it's extra motivation, general advice, or the answer to a specific question—turn to your Dream Team first. They're your champions, the ones you can count on to be by your side, even when the going gets tough. Keep in touch regularly by phone, in person, or by email. Share the progress you're making on your goals, ask for help and suggestions, and check in whenever problems come up. Your Dream Team is a first line of defense to help you troubleshoot even the toughest problem or the biggest case of procrastination!

Who might be on your Dream Team? If you've already filled out the "Help I Need" form, you've probably identified a few key people you can turn to again and again. If not, brainstorm possible helpers in your Goal Tracker. Now put stars by the three or four people you can absolutely count on to believe in you.

To recruit them, explain why you'd like their support and ask them if they'd be willing to be a member of your Dream Team. If someone says no, thank him or her for considering your request and move on to the next person on your list. Once you have a few willing people, write their names, addresses, phone numbers, and email addresses on form #14, "My Dream Team" (page 87), which you can photocopy for your Goal Tracker. With this information at your fingertips, you can get in touch with your Dream Team members whenever you need advice, motivation, or help.

Form #14
Date:

My Dream Team

Photocopy for your
Goal Tracker!!!

Name:_____

Address:_____

Phone number:_____

Email address:_____

Name:_____

Address:_____

Phone number:_____

Email address:_____

Name:_____

Address:_____

Phone number:_____

Email address:_____

Name:_____

Address:_____

Phone number:_____

Email address:_____

Don't Give Up

> "Before you begin a thing, remind yourself that difficulties and delays quite impossible to foresee are ahead. If you could see them clearly, naturally you could do a great deal to get rid of them, but you can't. You can only see one thing clearly and that is your goal. Form a mental vision of that and cling to it through thick and thin."
> —Kathleen Norris

How are you doing so far? Checking in is part of the goal-setting process, because along the way to your goal, you're learning a lot about yourself and what you're capable of. You're taking risks and facing challenges that may be very new to you. At times, you may feel totally energized by what you're trying to accomplish. But at other times, you may be overwhelmed, scared, or just plain stuck.

Some people get stuck so early in the process that they never get out of the starting blocks. Others find themselves sidelined by an unexpected problem. Still others get stuck just about the time they're ready to cross the finish line, like the racer who just doesn't have that final push. Do any of the following "I'm stuck" warning signs apply to you?

Sign #1: Procrastination. Are you putting off doing the things that would help you to move closer to your goal? (Read more about procrastination on pages 62–63.)

Sign #2: Distraction. When you finally decide that you're going to spend the afternoon working on your goal, do you find yourself doing all sorts of other things instead (talking to friends on the phone, hanging out in your room, playing video games, or *anything* except working on your goal)?

Sign #3: Boredom. When you think about your goal, do you practically start to fall asleep?

Sign #4: Goal? What Goal? Has it been weeks since you've even thought about your goal?

If any of these warning signs sound familiar, don't panic, despair, or give up. It's time to figure out what stands between you and your get-up-and-go:

1. **Check in with yourself.** Think back to when you first completed your Dreamprint (pages 29–31) and developed your goal. Try to remember how you felt. Were you excited, proud, happy, determined? What did you imagine yourself doing? Why was doing it important to you? Do you still want this goal? Maybe your life has changed since you set the goal. Maybe you realized after you started that the goal doesn't support your values. Maybe you figured out that it competes with another goal that's more important to you. Maybe you've realized that you're just too busy with everything else that's going on in your life. Whatever the reason, if this goal isn't for you, let it go and grab a new one. If, on the other hand, you're still committed to your goal, move on to the next check point.

2. **Check in with your goal.** If you still want to go after this goal, ask yourself if it's a SMART one—*savvy, measurable, active, reachable,* and *timed.* (See pages 36–38 for more about SMART goals.) Determine if you've set your goal too high or too low. If you expect too much from yourself, you might feel discouraged. If you expect too little—*yawn*—you won't care about the end result as much.

3. **Check in with your helpers or your Dream Team.** Look at the "Help I Need" and "My Dream Team" forms (pages 85 and 87). Did you ask for help and get it while climbing your Goal Ladder? Did you build a strong team to assist you along the way? Is there someone you can turn to for further support?

Depending on what you learn from your Goal Check, your goal may need a tune-up, some major adjustments, or a complete overhaul. Sometimes it may take a few tries to produce a Goal Ladder that works for you. No problem! That's why you can photocopy the "My Goal Ladder" form (page 52) as many times as you need to. The important thing is NOT to give up.

THINK IT & INK IT

Imagine that someone you admire has sent you a note praising you for not giving up. Use the journal section of your Goal Tracker to write yourself a note from that person's point of view.

GOAL GETTERS IN ACTION

Eleven-year-old **JOEY** was training to compete in a 10K "Race for the Cure" in honor of his grandmother, but then the unexpected happened. In the last soccer game of the season, he injured his knee in a midfield collision. He couldn't run for several weeks, which sunk his training schedule and shot his deadline. He was still committed to his goal, however, so he decided to give himself a new schedule—until the end of the summer—to run a different 10K race. Plus, he committed to running next year's "Race for the Cure."

When sixteen-year-old **PATTI** feels stuck, she asks herself if the goal is still important to her. "If it is, then I just psych myself up and do what it takes. If it's not, I change my goal. There are so many things I want to do that I don't have time to waste on things that are no longer important to me."

"I've always wanted to compete in the 100-meter butterfly in the Arizona state high school tournament," says **MICHAEL R.,** who's sixteen. "I almost made the tournament last year, when I took third in my region. However, only the top finisher went to state. Although I was disappointed, I didn't give up." Instead, Michael set a goal of cutting his time by one minute, which he hopes will earn him the privilege of competing in the state tournament next year.

Even when you've done everything you can, life has a way of throwing curve balls. These are times when your true character will be tested—times you're challenged to be greater, more positive, and more resourceful than you ever thought you could be.

For example, what happens if you've pursued your goal with all your heart but unexpected obstacles keep appearing in your path? It's easy to think, "I'm a failure" or "This is just too hard," and then put your dreams in a drawer. In fact, people do this every single day. Things may not turn out as you planned, but this doesn't mean you're a failure or that your goal isn't worthwhile. It can be very hard to persevere when times get tough, but that's what Goal Getters do. Adversity (misfortune) is only adversity until you find a way to turn it into opportunity.

Consider what these Goal Getters have to say about it:

"I believe you have to give 110 percent when it comes to achieving your goals. However, you have to learn when to step back and regroup. Everyone encounters obstacles at one time or another. If you let those obstacles derail you, you'll never reach your goals." PETTUS, 18

"I'm immensely stubborn. While this isn't always positive, it does help me achieve my goals, particularly when things get tough. I just never give up." PATTI, 16

"One goal I had from the day school started was to letter academically, which meant getting all A's or A-'s. At first, this seemed to be easily in my reach. But as the year progressed, I realized it wasn't going to be so easy. My enriched classes were harder than I expected. Rather than putting my goal in jeopardy, I gave up time with my friends so that I could spend more time studying." JESSICA, 15

"Just like everyone, I often run into obstacles. What helps me is to take a step back and do a reality check. Also, I talk with my friends who are in similar situations. This helps me put things into perspective and makes me realize that I'm not so alone." THIEN, 19

"I used to have a pretty bad temper and often created obstacles for myself because of it. I ended up in a lot of fights, and I eventually got thrown out of school. Now, I'm in a new school with new teachers. They've helped me work on keeping my temper under control and have taught me other ways to deal with my anger. As a result, I get along better with people. My grades are better, too." MICHAEL S., 17

"The way I've always overcome obstacles is by reminding myself that it's not just about seeing instant gratification. It's about the journey. For me, that means waking up with the hope of changing the world and continuing to work toward that and not give up—no matter what obstacles I run into." REBECCA, 18

 ## GOAL GETTERS IN ACTION

When **JENNIFER** was eleven, she was hit with one of the toughest trials anyone can face. "I'd just come off of a really good basketball season, and I was doing well in figure skating. I was competing a lot and began noticing a pain in the leg I landed my jumps on. At first I thought it was just growing pains or that I'd hurt my leg playing basketball. I started wearing a brace, but that didn't help. After about a month, my mom took me to see our family doctor. Although she wasn't overly concerned, she ordered an X-ray. When we got the results, we were shocked. I had bone cancer in my leg."

Jennifer had surgery the next day, but that was only the start of what would turn out to be a life-changing experience. After recovering from the surgery, Jennifer began nearly a year of chemotherapy, which meant being hospitalized for a week every month. Jennifer remembers, "The chemotherapy was really intense because of how sick it made me, but the physical therapy was by far the toughest part."

Basically, Jennifer had to learn to walk all over again. "When I started therapy, my leg had been in a cast for nearly six months, and I couldn't even bend it." Jennifer started small, just putting weight on her leg and bending her knee. Then she set more ambitious goals: walking with crutches, walking with a cane, and finally walking on her own. "It sounds so simple now," she says, "but at the time it was a tremendous amount of work."

Along the way, Jennifer had to accept the fact that she wasn't ever going to be able to skate or play basketball again. "Giving up sports—particularly basketball, because it meant giving up my dream of playing in high school and going to the state tournament—was really hard. But I realized giving up sports didn't mean I had to give up setting goals. It just meant I had to change my goals. At first this was really hard, but as time went on, sports seemed so much less important than they had when I was first diagnosed. I realized that there are so many other things I want to do with my life—things that are far more important than playing basketball. This certainly didn't happen overnight, but I did come to realize that my life wasn't going to end just because I couldn't play basketball."

Jennifer starting trying a lot of new things: golf and swimming (the only sports her doctor would let her play), her school youth group, and the school yearbook. She also realized that through her experience she could help others. "When I was sick, I saw so many kids who were sicker than me," she says. "I felt lucky, and when I got better, I wanted to help them." After considering her options, Jennifer got involved with Encourage, a group of teen survivors of life-threatening illnesses who each work with two or three other teens who are sick, offering them advice, raising their spirits, and acting as role models. She even spearheaded the group's efforts to raise forty thousand dollars so members could develop a Web site, including a chat room where a teen survivor is available for an hour each night to answer kids' questions.

One of the ways Jennifer kept herself motivated through the toughest hours of her cancer treatments was by reading the words of Mary Tyler Moore: "Pain nourishes courage. You can't be brave if you've only had wonderful things happen to you." Jennifer says, "I learned that life can be difficult at times, but when bad things happen it's an opportunity to see life in a new way. And a chance to really develop your courage."

Here are a handful of strategies to help you overcome what stands in your way. Try them out and see what works best for you.

Strategy 1: Take control where you can. Unexpected circumstances, stress, and your own emotions can undermine your feelings of control. With lots going on in your life, it's easy to feel anxious and overwhelmed. That's why Goal Ladders focus on one *step* at a time—and why life is lived one *day* at a time. There's only so much you (or anyone) can do.

Sure, things happen that you don't expect and you can't control. But there's one thing you always have control over: your reaction. You can make a conscious choice not to let unforeseen circumstances or adversity get the best of you. Here are some tips that can help:

- Focus on being positive, caring, and compassionate. If you feel yourself ready to react out of anger, stop and take a deep breath. Think of one good thing about the situation you're in.

- If things don't turn out as you'd hoped, focus on what you learned in the process. You may not reach the goal you went after originally, but what *did* you reach? What did you learn that you didn't know before?

- Appreciate what you've accomplished. It's easy to focus solely on what you still want instead of appreciating where you are today. Give yourself credit for how far you've gotten.

- Remember that what others think about you is less important than what *you* think about you. Even if you're a little disappointed, don't be too hard on yourself, and don't assume that other people think you've failed. Treat yourself with the respect and kindness that you'd show a friend in your situation.

- Keep looking for opportunities and new ways to troubleshoot problems. Things may not be working, but a solution might be right under your nose. Have you looked there lately?

When you're under a lot of stress, the most important goal is to take care of yourself. You may need to give yourself a vacation from your goals until you feel ready to give them a try again. In fact, you may even want to set a few "Anti Goals." Here are some real-life Anti Goals used and recommended by other teens:

- Sleep in as late as possible one weekend a month.

- Spend twenty minutes each day doing absolutely nothing.

- Throw your clothes on the floor for an entire weekend and leave the clean-up for Monday.

- Rent your favorite video, invite some friends over, and laugh until your stomach hurts.

Do any of these Anti Goals appeal to you? Give them a try, if they do. Or you can come up with some of your own Anti Goals. Write them in your Goal Tracker to remind yourself that goal setting isn't something you have to do twenty-four hours a day, seven days a week.

Strategy 2: Inspire yourself with words. When you're reading or listening to an interview with your favorite celebrity, watch for those lines that make you say, "Wow!" Calendars, books of quotations, Web sites—inspiring words are everywhere once you start looking. Find that special quote that speaks to you and your situation; you'll know it when you see it. When you find it, write it in your Goal Tracker, so you'll see it often. You can even write it on an index card and carry it with you in your wallet or backpack, or tape it to the inside of your locker.

On form #15, "Quotes To-Go" (page 97), is a collection of quotations that you can use for inspiration anytime. You can photocopy the page, cut out the quotes you like best, and carry them with you. Or you can glue them anywhere in your Goal Tracker. You could even have them laminated at a copy center, if you'd like.

Photocopy for your
Goal Tracker!!!

Quotes To-Go

"There is no such thing as failure.
Mistakes happen in your life to bring into
focus more clearly who you are."—Oprah Winfrey

"I've always felt that within myself,
I can find a way to win."—Joe Montana

"All that is necessary to break the spell of inertia
and frustration is this: act as if it were impossible
to fail. That is the talisman, the formula, the command
of right-about-face that turns us from failure
toward success."—Dorothea Brande

"Too many of us are hung up on what we don't have,
can't have, or won't ever have. We spend too much
energy being down, when we could use that same energy—
if not less of it—doing, or at least trying to do, some
of the things we really want to do."—Terry McMillan

"I've missed more than nine thousand shots in my career.
Twenty-six times I've been trusted to take the game
winning shot and missed. I've failed over and over
and over again in my life. And that is why
I succeed."—Michael Jordan

Strategy 3: Learn from role models. Another great way to inspire yourself is by learning about other successful Goal Getters—people who started their own businesses, raised money for causes they believe in, starred in their own plays, or landed their dream jobs. Whatever you're interested in doing, you can find inspiring role models by reading about where others got their ideas, how they made a start, and how they got past the roadblocks. Look for interviews with or biographies of the role models who make you sit up and take notice.

So how do you pick an effective role model? Not everyone makes a great role model. Your role models should be people who can teach you and motivate you to become better than you ever thought you could be. How do you find these kinds of people? Here are three tips:

- Pick a role model who's doing or has already done what you want to do. You can learn from someone else's experience instead of having to "invent the wheel" all on your own.

- Choose someone who has values similar to yours. Take another look at your completed form #3, "Values That Matter to Me" (pages 20–21). Who shares those same values? Who believes in the things you believe in? Find role models who share your views and inspire your mind and heart.

- Watch for someone whose life is in balance—an all-around good role model—not someone who's a superstar in one area or who has let you down with behaviors you don't agree with.

Strategy 4: Surround yourself with supporters. Hanging out with people who are seeking the same goals can give you an amazing boost. You can encourage each other to think in new ways and overcome your hurdles. With the help of understanding friends, you can find the courage to take risks you might not be willing to take on your own. Together, you may be able to accomplish more than any of you could alone. Your buddies can be family members, friends, classmates, coworkers, neighbors, or members of your Dream Team (see pages 86–87). Choose anyone with whom you share a common goal.

Strategy 5: Chart your progress. Sometimes you're not really as stuck as you think you may be. This is why charting your progress is so important when setting goals. When you know how you're doing—especially when you're doing well—you'll naturally want to do even better. And if you're not making as much progress as you'd hoped, you'll be able to do something about it, instead of giving up.

The most effective progress markers are visual (you notice them), creative (they're fun), and updated often (so you can track your efforts). When climbing your Goal Ladder, mark it up so you know what you've accomplished. Put big stars by steps you've completed, for example, or write "Way to go!" You could even highlight each completed rung in a different color.

If you've been trying to climb a particular rung and just can't seem to move forward, stop and ask yourself what's going on. Do you need some support? Some tools you hadn't thought of before? Some more time? Give yourself what you need to keep making progress. You'll thank yourself later!

Strategy 6: Do *whatever* works. Are you totally fed up, tired out, and ready to give up? Have you used all of the strategies but *still* can't seem to get anywhere? Try some or all of these ideas:

- Find someone you can count on to pump you up or feed your ego, and go to him or her for an emergency pick-me-up. Sometimes just hearing someone say, "I believe in you" is enough to get you through.

- Invite your friends over for a pity party. Designate a set amount of time during which you can complain, moan, and groan to each other. Then, when your time's up, that's it. Have some fun and encourage each other to get back on track.

- Think of the law of inertia. A body at rest tends to stay at rest; a body in motion tends to stay in motion. So, even if you're not sure what to do, do *something*. Taking one step, no matter how small, may be enough to get you moving again.

- If you haven't already gotten the get-there, know-how, or feel-good help you need (see pages 78–81), ask for it now. If your goal is important to you, don't be afraid to get the assistance you need.

TRUTH TIME: Sometimes, no matter how hard you try, you won't get to your goal. It can happen to anybody—even the most famous Goal Getters you can think of. Goal setting involves taking risks, and with risks, there's always a chance of a letdown.

Not reaching a goal can be a painful experience, especially if you've put lots of energy into the process. It's natural to feel disappointed and upset. You may spend lots of time going over what went wrong and what you could have done differently. You may catch yourself repeatedly saying, "If only . . ." and imagining a better outcome than the one you experienced. Dwelling on "If onlys" doesn't get you very far. Keep in mind that you showed a great deal of courage and perseverance to try as hard as you did. And know that you learned something—about yourself, your dreams, and your goals—along the way. With these thoughts in mind, you can find that inner strength to set a new goal that's wiser and has a better chance of success. You owe it to yourself to keep moving forward, instead of focusing too much on the past.

Remember, everyone fails or makes mistakes at some point. It's part of being human. In fact, the only sure way of never experiencing failure is by *not doing anything*. But is that what you really want . . . to hide from life and avoid any risks? The player who sits out every game doesn't have to worry about missing a shot—or making the winning shot. The singer who never performs in front of a crowd never has to worry about missing a note—or getting applause. To get the rewards in life, you've got to be a part of the action. And that means getting back up again after a fall.

It may be helpful to do a "Goal Check" to help you assess your goal and the outcome. You can photocopy form #16 on pages 101–102 and fill it out to review your efforts. Like a post-game recap, a "Goal Check" will help you determine what worked and what didn't—good fuel for the future.

Form #16
Date: _____

Goal Check

Photocopy for your
Goal Tracker!!!

My goal was:_____

_____

Result I wanted:_____

_____

Result I got:_____

_____

Did I have:	If no, what did I need that I didn't get?
Get-there help? ❑ yes ❑ no	
Know-how help? ❑ yes ❑ no	
Feel-good help? ❑ yes ❑ no	
A Dream Team? ❑ yes ❑ no	
Enough time, given the other things going on in my life? ❑ yes ❑ no	

$\longrightarrow$

What would have helped me reach my goal that I didn't know before?

Would I have a better chance of getting to this goal at a different time of year? (For example, in the summer instead of the end of a school term.) ❑ yes   ❑ no   If yes, when?

Do I want to try this goal again? ❑ yes   ❑ no   If yes, when?

What have I learned that will help me with my other goals in the future?

The results of your "Goal Check" will tell you something about yourself and the goal you set out to achieve. What you do with this information is up to you. Many Goal Getters have already learned that persistence and perseverance are the main ingredients for success. You can learn this, too!

If you find that:	Try this:
You set your goal to please someone else.	Go back to your Goal Tracker to review all you've written about your values and dreams. Select a new goal that truly reflects your own ambitions and desires.
Your goal is too easy.	Make it more challenging by asking yourself to accomplish more or by tightening the deadlines. This way, you'll stay more inspired and won't decide, "Why bother?"
Your goal is too hard.	Break your big goal into smaller, more manageable goals. Focus on creating goals that are SMART (see pages 36–38).
Your goal is outside your control.	Write a new goal that depends on *you*—and no one but you—to complete it.
You're too busy.	Change your deadlines to give yourself more time, or give yourself permission to put it off until you're not so busy.
You're feeling stressed out.	Make it your number one goal to *take care of yourself*. Give yourself a break for a few days, while you focus on eating right, exercising, and getting some rest. Then, when you feel calmer, decide whether you're ready to pursue the goal again or set a different one.
You're not getting the help or support you need.	Figure out exactly what you need and who can help. And then reach out!

Form #17
Date: _____

Conversation Starters

Photocopy for your
Goal Tracker!!!

Ask these questions of friends, family members, or other people in your life.

- Do you procrastinate? What advice do you have for overcoming procrastination?

- When things go wrong, how do you keep yourself thinking positively?

- What do you do to boost your self-confidence?

- When you need help, who do you turn to?

- Suppose you could speak to a famous person, living or dead, who could help you with your goal. Who would it be? What would you ask?

- Do you have a mentor? How does your mentor help you?

- Can you think of anyone who'd be able to help me reach my goal? Anyone who'd be a good mentor for me?

- What kinds of adversity have you faced in your life? What advice do you have for overcoming obstacles?

- Have you ever failed at something? How did you handle this?

Keep Believing in Yourself

"I've always believed that you can think positive just as well as you can think negative."—Sugar Ray Robinson

No matter where you are on your Goal Ladder at this moment, you're still the person you were when you started—full of potential. Maybe you've climbed a few rungs and you're feeling great: keep up the good work! Maybe you've gotten halfway there and you're not sure how to proceed: keep going by making sure that you've got the support you need. Maybe you've hit some obstacles or perhaps even experienced failure, and you're not sure where to go from here. Whatever you do, don't stop. You have the power to reach your potential—and stay positive every step of the way.

Part 4

CELEBRATE YOUR SUCCESS

Reward Yourself

All your hard work deserves a reward. Appreciating and applauding your own efforts helps keep you motivated and marks those moments when you're on top of the world. Savor that feeling of accomplishment when you're able to look at your Goal Ladder and say, "I made it!" Learning how to reward yourself is one of the most fun parts of goal setting.

Most people think about rewards only for reaching a goal. But it's just as important to reward yourself for little steps you make day by day—even if you don't get your goal in the end. In fact, that's the biggest difference between successful Goal Getters and others. Goal Getters remember that it's the journey that matters, not the instant satisfaction of getting what you want when you want it. Some days, you may feel that you're not making much progress, but if you stay focused and true to yourself, no matter what, you'll always have something to be proud of. Your courage and your belief in yourself will grow—and that's an accomplishment (and reward) in itself.

Rewards can come from two places: you or other people. You're in control of the rewards you give yourself. Some teens reward themselves with a break or a fun present. For example, fifteen-year-old Eric rewards himself by playing with his pet snake whenever he finishes his homework. Sixteen-year-old Michael R. gives himself the weekend off from studying if he's made his study goals all week. Fifteen-year-old Meghan eats a bowl of double-fudge-brownie ice cream after she cleans her room. Fifteen-year-old Amanda rewards herself by putting money in her savings account whenever she gets a paycheck.

Rewards from other people are the icing on the cake. The smile from the kid you tutor, a high-five from a teammate, words of praise from your coach, encouragement from your parents and teachers, a celebration with your friends—these rewards are special because they show that people appreciate you and what you do. If your supporters want to help you celebrate your goal, let them! And when people you know give you the praise you deserve, savor it.

"My favorite reward is to see others proud of me."
CHRISTINA, 12

"When I achieve my goal, I feel so good about myself! And then I start working on a new goal." PATTI, 16

"When I do something my parents are proud of, they tell me so and that makes me feel good about myself." ARTURO, 13

THINK IT & INK IT

In the journal section of your Goal Tracker, make a congratulations card for yourself, decorating it any way you wish. Be sure that it says how proud you are of all that you've accomplished.

GOAL GETTERS IN ACTION

BETH, eighteen, remembers, "I had my heart set on going to Notre Dame, but I knew it was a pretty ambitious goal. When I got accepted, I was so excited. So were my parents. They took me out to dinner at my favorite restaurant. They also bought me a bouquet of carnations dyed gold and blue to match Notre Dame's colors, and framed my letter of acceptance and hung it in my room."

MICHAEL R., sixteen, negotiated his reward ahead of time. "My parents have always stressed the importance of good grades, but they've mainly focused on the long term. They've never been the type to give me money for getting A's. But they do help motivate me and are committed to helping me celebrate my success. When I turned sixteen, they helped me buy a BMW. Not a new one, but an '88. I'd wanted one for as long as I can remember. They paid part, and I paid the rest. For me, there couldn't have been a better reward."

Seventeen-year-old DREW was named one of ten national "Spirit of Community" leaders by the Prudential company for his work starting Harvest House, a permanent soup kitchen in his area. He says, "The recognition is nice, but it's not why I do it. I do it because there are people in my community who are hungry and because I realize that, even though I'm still in high school, I have the power to make a difference."

JENNIFER, age sixteen, has received many public rewards for her work on behalf of children with serious illnesses. How does she feel about the recognition? "I know how lucky I am to be a cancer survivor, and I want to do everything I can to help others as a way of saying thank you to those who helped me. Knowing that I've helped someone else through a tough time is the best reward I could ever receive."

Have you ever noticed that some rewards mean more to you than others? Rewards have to fit who you are, what you like, and what you've accomplished. Think about the reward you last gave yourself:

- **Was it meaningful to you?** First and foremost, rewards must be meaningful—and motivating—to *you*. Find rewards that click with what you like. Just as goals are unique to each individual, so are rewards. What motivates your best friend may put you right to sleep.

- **Was it fair considering what you did to get it?** Keep your rewards consistent with your goals—major accomplishments deserve more significant rewards. You may decide to take an afternoon off if you make your study goals all week. But if you make your study goals all *semester*, you may want to ask your mom or dad about taking a weekend trip to the beach.

- **Were you focused on why you got the reward?** Was the reward for the three hours you spent on your history report, or for finishing it? Was the reward for scoring five points in the game, or for not fouling out? You'll feel the power of the reward more deeply if you know exactly what you did to get it.

- **Did the reward come at the right time?** Every step that you take toward your goal is a cause for celebration. And rewards should be frequent enough to remind you of your achievements. Don't put off rewards for too long. If you're buying yourself a new magazine because you did all your chores around the house, go out and get it as soon as you can—not next week or next month.

Here are some ways other teens suggest celebrating goals:

1. Share the news with friends, family, and your Dream Team (see pages 86–87). Let them know how proud you are of what you've done—and you'll see how proud they are of you.

2. Keep a record of your accomplishments in your Goal Tracker, including the goals you reach, the honors you receive, and the compliments you get. While you may think that you'll always remember what it feels like to reach your goal, memories fade. Writing things down gives you something to look back on— a way of reminding yourself often of all you've achieved.

3. Write a letter to yourself. Describe the goal you set, why you set it, what you did to achieve it, and what you're doing to celebrate it. Add the letter to your Goal Tracker.

4. Paint a picture or write a poem or song to celebrate your success.

5. Throw a party or host a picnic for your friends.

6. Make a special cake for a family dinner and write "I got my goal!" on the icing.

7. If you have goal-setting buddies, find out when they plan to reach their goals and celebrate together—go to the movies or a game, have a sleepover, or go camping.

8. Give something to someone in need. This can give you the boost you deserve—and help someone else at the same time.

Take a few minutes to brainstorm the rewards that would be most meaningful to you. To get started, think about:

- the kinds of things you like to have

- the things you love to do

- hobbies you like to spend time doing

- who you like to spend your time with and what you like to do together

- how you like to get away from it all

- what makes you feel proud or happy

- what gift you'd most like to receive

- how you'd spend five, ten, or twenty dollars if you found it

THINK IT & INK IT

Take some time to look through both sections of your Goal Tracker, particularly the first several forms and journal pages. How do you feel now about the hopes and dreams you expressed then? Write in the journaling section about where you are today in relation to those hopes and dreams. Are you happy with the progress you've made toward your goal? If not, are there steps you can take now that will move you closer to it? If you *are* satisfied with yourself, write about those feelings. Boast a little, if you want. (Remember, no one has to read what you wrote!)

On page 114 is form #18, "I've Earned It!" You can photocopy it, fill it out, and store it in your Goal Tracker as a reminder that rewards are a fun and meaningful way to celebrate your progress and your success.

You probably love it when other people notice how hard you've worked. What about giving others the same support? You can easily offer your congratulations or say, "That was great!" Here are some other ways to be a part of the celebration:

- When a friend reaches a goal, ask if you can spread the news. If your friend agrees, let others know about it.

- Write a letter to your school or local newspaper telling about your friend's achievements.

- Send a card saying how proud you are of your friend's accomplishment. Cards are easy to buy, make by hand, or create on a computer.

- Tape a "Congratulations!" or "Way to go!" banner to your friend's locker.

Form #18
Date:
_____

I've Earned It!

Photocopy for your
Goal Tracker!!!

When I do this . . .	I'll reward myself with . . .

Form #19
Date:
_____

Conversation Starters

Photocopy for your
Goal Tracker!!!

Ask these questions of friends, family members, or other people in your life.

• When you set and achieve a goal, what do you do to celebrate?

• When people you know meet their goals, how do you recognize their achievements?

• If you ever feel like giving up on your goals, what do you do?

• What's the most meaningful reward you've ever received? What was it for? How did you feel when you got it?

• Knowing me, what kinds of rewards do you think would be meaningful to me?

• If I achieve my goal of _____, would you be willing to help me celebrate my success? If so, how?

• The next time you achieve a goal, what can I do to help you celebrate your success?

The End Is Really the Beginning

"Reach high, for stars lie hidden in
your soul. Dream deep, for every dream
precedes the goal."—Pamela Vaull Starr

After you've taken a few deep breaths and enjoyed the view from the top of your Goal Ladder, where do you go from there? Most likely, you'll have other goals that you're just as motivated to work toward, and you may feel it's time to get moving again. Life is a continuous process of recognizing your dreams, setting goals that can help make your dreams real, and then taking action every day to get there. There's never any moment of being "finished" because we're always growing and changing, dreaming new dreams, and figuring out our goals. Feeling revved up and totally focused one day, stuck or side-tracked the next, are the normal ups and downs of the goal-setting process. When you look back a month from now, six months from now, or a year from now, you'll see just how far you've come.

You're unstoppable as long as you keep taking the next step. Allow yourself to imagine how you'll feel when you have what you really want and are living the life of your dreams. Why wait one more day to begin living it? Are you ready? Go for it!

GOAL-GETTER RESOURCES

 ## Books
(Nonfiction)

Awaken the Olympian Within: Stories from America's Greatest Olympic Motivators compiled by John Naber (Torrance, CA: Griffin Publishing Group, 1998). This collection of 27 inspirational essays is written by many of America's most successful motivational speakers. The authors share more than 30 Olympic gold medals and 57 medals overall. Their stories of focus, confidence, persistence, and success serve as great inspiration to anyone striving to be their best.

Beat Procrastination and Make the Grade: The Six Styles of Procrastination and How Students Can Overcome Them by Linda Sapadin with Jack Maguire (New York: Penguin USA, 1999). This book identifies six styles of procrastination and offers a specific program for each style designed to help students unlearn self-destructive behaviors and realize their full academic potential.

Creative Visualization: Use the Power of Your Imagination to Create What You Want in Your Life by Shakti Gawain (Novato, CA: New World Library, 1995). This guide teaches methods that are practical and easy to use in daily life. Learn how to use the power of your imagination to change negative habits, improve your self-esteem, experience deep relaxation, and achieve the goals you've set for yourself.

Gutsy Girls: Young Women Who Dare by Tina Schwager and Michele Schuerger (Minneapolis: Free Spirit Publishing Inc., 1999). Read the inspiring stories of 25 young women who experienced daring feats and accomplished history-making achievements ranging from drag racing to sky diving to climbing Mt. McKinley. Their stories will inspire both girls and boys as the young women discuss what they had to overcome to reach their goals.

How We Made the World a Better Place: Kids and Teens Write on How They Changed Their Corner of the World by the staff of Fairview Press (Minneapolis: Fairview Press, 1998). In 1997, Fairview Press sponsored a writing contest challenging kids and teens to write how they felt about something they'd done to change the world. The responses—from groups that helped clothe the homeless to a Girl Scout troop that sponsored families in need during the holidays—will inspire you to take a look at how you can make positive changes in your community.

Making Every Day Count: Daily Readings for Young People on Solving Problems, Setting Goals, & Feeling Good About Yourself by Pamela Espeland and Elizabeth Verdick (Minneapolis: Free Spirit Publishing Inc., 1998). A year's worth of daily inspiration, affirmation, and advice helps you face challenges, plan for the future, and appreciate your wonderful and unique qualities.

Mentoring Heroes: 52 Fabulous Women's Paths to Success and the Mentors Who Empowered Them by Mary K. Doyle (Geneva, IL: 3E Press, 2000). We don't get anywhere totally on our own. We sometimes need a little help from an experienced friend. The 52 successful women in this book got to where they are today with the assistance of such friends and mentors and share their stories about the men and women who mentored them.

The Myths and Realities of Goal Setting: Guidelines for Designing an Extraordinary Life! by Gary Ryan Blair (Tarpon Springs, FL: The GoalsGuy, 1999). How you think about goals and success affects how much you're able to accomplish. This book addresses the 15 common myths that can get in the way of that progress.

The Person Who Changed My Life: Prominent Americans Recall Their Mentors edited by Matilda Raffa Cuomo (Secaucus, NJ: Carol Publishing Group, 1999). This is a collection of essays in which individuals who have distinguished themselves in their fields write about the men and women who served as their mentors. Among the contributors are Walter Cronkite, Larry King, Dr. Arthur Caliandro, Elie Wiesel, Marian Wright Edelman, Julia Child, Gloria Estefan, and Dina Merrill.

The 7 Habits of Highly Effective Teens: The Ultimate Teenage Success Guide by Sean Covey (New York: Simon & Schuster, 2000). The Seven Habits provide a step-by-step guide to help you improve your self-esteem, build friendships, resist peer pressure, achieve your goals, get along with your parents, and more.

Teens With Courage to Give: Young People Who Triumphed Over Tragedy and Volunteered to Make a Difference by Jackie Waldman (Berkeley, CA: Conari Press, 2000). This book profiles 30 young people who have overcome great odds to reach out and help others. First-person accounts include an amputee running the Paralympics and the son of a cancer patient creating support groups for kids with parents who are ill.

Tuesdays with Morrie: An Old Man, a Young Man and Life's Greatest Lesson by Mitch Ablom (New York: Doubleday, 1996). The true story of how award-winning sports columnist Mitch Ablom reconnected with an old professor who played the role of spiritual mentor one final time, dispensing wisdom as he lay dying of Lou Gehrig's Disease (ALS).

What Teens Need to Succeed: Proven, Practical Ways to Shape Your Own Future by Peter L. Benson, Judy Galbraith, and Pamela Espeland (Minneapolis: Free Spirit Publishing Inc., 1998). Based on a nation-wide survey, this book describes 40 developmental "assets" all teens need to succeed in life, then gives you hundreds of ideas for building assets at home, at school, in the community, and with friends.

Write Where You Are: How to Use Writing to Make Sense of Your Life by Caryn Mirriam-Goldberg (Minneapolis: Free Spirit Publishing Inc., 1999). This book helps you articulate your hopes and dreams, your life and possibilities, through writing.

Books
(Fiction)

The Contender by Robert Lipsyte (New York: HarperCollins, 1991). In this inspiring novel, a young man, Alfred Brooks, struggles against the pitfalls of his life in Harlem—drugs, crime, violence, and poverty—and learns important life lessons while on the path to becoming a champion boxer.

Danger Zone by David Klass (New York: Scholastic Paperbacks, 1998). Read this award-winning sports novel to find out how young basketball star Jimmy Doyle prevails over a number of obstacles including racism and neo-Nazi threats as a member of America's teen "dream team" in European play-offs.

Mama I Want to Sing by Vy Higginsen with Tonya Bolden (New York: Scholastic, 1992). The 1940s African-American heroine of this book becomes the star of the Mt. Calvary Full Gospel Church choir and decides to pursue her dream of singing professionally. Her determination in the face of adversity leads to her success as a pop star with a Broadway smash.

Necessary Roughness by Marie G. Lee (New York: HarperCollins, 1996). The story focuses on Chan Jung Kim, a Korean-American high school senior who moves from Los Angeles to small-town Minnesota. In L.A., Chan was his school's soccer star and a member of a larger Korean-American community; in small-town Minnesota, he finds himself playing a new sport, facing the prejudices of a town that's never seen an Asian-American family before, and torn between the dictates of his traditional father and the demands of his football teammates.

The New You by Kathleen Leverich (New York: Greenwillow, 1999). Juggling a new haircut, a new home, and a new school, Abigail wrestles with issues of self-esteem, fitting in, and friendship, while she searches for a new identity.

Pay It Forward: A Novel by Catherine Ryan Hyde (New York: Simon & Schuster, 2000). "Think of an idea for world change, and put it into action." That's the school assignment Trevor tries to fulfill by creating a new twist on the pyramid scheme. He decides to do three good deeds stipulating that each of the people he helps do likewise.

 # Organizations

Big Brothers Big Sisters of America
230 North 13 Street
Philadelphia, PA 19107
(215) 567-7000
www.bbbsa.org
Big Brothers Big Sisters of America provides one-to-one mentoring relationships between adult volunteers and children primarily from single-parent families.

The GoalsGuy
911 Klosterman Road East
Tarpon Springs, FL 34689
1-877-462-5748
www.goalsguy.com
The GoalsGuy is a company that provides resources and seminars on goal setting. Click on the Knowledge section at the Web site to read several tips and ideas about how to set and achieve your goals.

Independent Means
126 Powers Avenue
Santa Barbara, CA 93103
www.independentmeans.com
Independent Means Inc. is a company that provides a variety of services and products aimed at advancing financial independence for women under twenty. This includes economic education and encouraging relationships to develop between the teens and adult entrepreneurs and mentors. Camp $tart-Up teaches attendees how to develop their own business plans.

National Mentoring Partnership

1600 Duke Street, Suite 300

Alexandria, VA 22314

(703) 224-2200

www.mentoring.org

The National Mentoring Partnership works with local organizations to improve and expand mentoring programs throughout the United States. For more information, contact the national office or visit the Web site for a listing of organizations in your area.

YMCA of the U.S.A.

Association Advancement

101 North Wacker Drive

Chicago, IL 60606

(312) 977-0031

www.ymca.net

YMCAs are the largest not-for-profit community service organizations in America. They work to meet the health and social service needs of 17.5 million men, women, and children. YMCAs are for people of all faiths, races, abilities, ages, and incomes. Call to ask about mentoring programs.

Youth Venture

1700 North Moore Street, Suite 2000

Arlington, VA 22209

703-527-4126

www.youthventure.org

Youth Venture challenges young people to define their goals, to demonstrate how their efforts will strengthen themselves and their communities, and to create plans for achieving them. Youth Venture provides the support network that young people need to launch and run their own ventures that will bring positive change to their schools and communities. For more information, check out the Web site or contact the national headquarters listed above.

YWCA of the U.S.A.
Empire State Building
350 Fifth Avenue, Suite 301
New York, NY 10118
(212) 273-7800
www.ywca.org
The YWCA empowers women and girls by offering a wide range of services and programs (including mentoring) that enrich and transform their lives. Check out its Web site for more information and to find a YWCA near you.

 # Web Sites

eGroups About-Motivation
www.egroups.com/group/About-Motivation
Each week a new motivational quote is delivered to you via email to provide you with instruction, training, and encouragement in the areas of motivation, self-improvement, and personal growth. Check out this Web page to find out how to subscribe.

Northwestern University's Career Services
www.stuaff.nwu.edu/ucs/Students/started/goalset.htm
Northwestern University's Career Services Web site has a page devoted to goal setting. It offers tips on setting goals as well as additional links and resources.

Review.com
The Princeton Review
2315 Broadway
New York, NY 10024
1-800-273-8439
www.review.com
Review.com is part of The Princeton Review, a leading test preparation organization. The Web site is a great source of online information for teens and young adults seeking college, graduate school, and career information. It offers students information about standardized tests, admissions, internships, and career programs.

Top Achievement
www.topachievement.com
Top Achievement is a Web site that offers The Personal Achievement Quote of the Day, resources, a discussion board, articles, and more to help you get motivated, set and achieve your goals, and focus on self-improvement.

INDEX

ACKNOWLEDGMENTS

I've dreamed of writing this book since I was a little girl. I worked hard on it, but I couldn't have written it without the love, laughter, and support of many people—family, friends, colleagues, and some people I've never even met—who were willing to help me just because I asked. I owe you all my sincerest thanks.

I would like to thank the following people in particular:

All the teens I interviewed who eagerly shared their hopes and dreams, and provided me with so much inspiration.

My editors, Jana Branch and Elizabeth Verdick, and everyone at Free Spirit—including Judy Galbraith, Margie Lisovskis, Darsi Dreyer, and Marieka Heinlen—for their hard work and relentless efforts to make this book the best it could possibly be.

Caryn Pernu, who first believed me capable of writing it.

LoAnn and Bill Mockler, for a decade of support and for suggesting (repeatedly) that I call Free Spirit.

Bob Bartikoski, for seeing me as the author and artist I want to be.

Patty Cagwin, my college writing partner and first forever friend, for her long-distance love and support.

Bunny Robinson, who gave me my first job as a writer; Colleen Kaney, the best networker I know; and Colleen Frankhart, with whom I've shared so many deadlines, for teaching me so much about writing and friendship.

Steve Williams and Mary Jeub, for being the best clients-turned-friends a corporate writer could ask for.

Princess Peggy Peterson, whose annual girls' weekend changed my life, and who always knows how to reach across the miles and touch my heart just when I need it most.

Diane Wolter, for being my most frequent travel companion and for enriching my life in so many ways.

Shawn Dooley, for helping me improve my golf game and for being such a wonderful friend.

Tess Nelson and Lynn Barber, my Dream Team and personal cheerleaders, who have helped inspire my passions and been at my side when I needed it most.

Fellow writer and dreamer Cathy Madison, who has always seen so much more in me than I've seen in myself.

My neighbor Jill Griffiths, who has taught me much about small and large kindnesses of the heart.

My every-other-Friday "Egg and I" breakfast group—Anna Giacomini, Jack Jerome, Nancy Meyers, Mame Osteen, Laurie Phillips, and Cathy Spengler—for wonderful conversation and constant encouragement.

Fellow Idea Girls Mary Ness, Marianne Richmond, Molly Scheer, Joann Hall Swenson, and Joyce Willman, for believing in my idea and for supporting me and one another as we pursue our dreams.

My surrogate mothers Caroline Scott, Irene Zylla, and Anne Stokowski, for reminding me of how blessed I am to be part of such large and loving families.

And finally, Steve Stokowski, who has loved and believed in me since I was a teen, and my sisters Karen Carlson, Susann Bachel, Diane Hawe, and Mary Bachel, with whom I first learned to set goals in pursuit of my dreams. I would be so much less today without their love and support.

ABOUT THE AUTHOR

© Ann Marsden

Beverly Bachel is a writer, artist, consultant, and business owner who attributes her success to her ability to set goals, a skill she learned the summer she sold her first pitcher of lemonade. The founder of a communications consulting firm, she has written for dozens of Fortune 500 companies and numerous publications. In addition, she is the founder of Idea Girls, a group of entrepreneurs dedicated to developing products that inspire others to pursue their dreams and use their talents to make positive changes in the world.